# Scrap-Basket
## STRIPS AND SQUARES

### Quilting with 2½", 5", and 10" Treasures

### KIM BRACKETT

Scrap-Basket Strips and Squares:
Quilting with 2½", 5", and 10" Treasures
© 2016 by Kim Brackett

Martingale®
19021 120th Ave. NE, Ste. 102
Bothell, WA 98011-9511 USA
ShopMartingale.com

No part of this product may be reproduced in any form, unless otherwise stated, in which case reproduction is limited to the use of the purchaser. The written instructions, photographs, designs, projects, and patterns are intended for the personal, noncommercial use of the retail purchaser and are under federal copyright laws; they are not to be reproduced by any electronic, mechanical, or other means, including informational storage or retrieval systems, for commercial use. Permission is granted to photocopy patterns for the personal use of the retail purchaser. Attention teachers: Martingale encourages you to use this book for teaching, subject to the restrictions stated above.

The information in this book is presented in good faith, but no warranty is given nor results guaranteed. Since Martingale has no control over choice of materials or procedures, the company assumes no responsibility for the use of this information.

Printed in China
21 20 19 18 17        8 7 6 5 4 3 2

Library of Congress Cataloging-in-Publication Data is available upon request.

ISBN: 978-1-60468-670-8

## MISSION STATEMENT

We empower makers who use fabric and yarn to make life more enjoyable.

## CREDITS

**PUBLISHER AND CHIEF VISIONARY OFFICER**
Jennifer Erbe Keltner

**CONTENT DIRECTOR**
Karen Costello Soltys

**DESIGN MANAGER**
Adrienne Smitke

**MANAGING EDITOR**
Tina Cook

**PRODUCTION MANAGER**
Regina Girard

**ACQUISITIONS EDITOR**
Karen M. Burns

**PHOTOGRAPHER**
Brent Kane

**TECHNICAL EDITOR**
Nancy Mahoney

**ILLUSTRATOR**
Anne Moscicki

**COPY EDITOR**
Tiffany Mottet

# CONTENTS

INTRODUCTION  4
THINGS TO KNOW ABOUT PRECUTS  5
SPECIAL PIECING TECHNIQUES  7

## PROJECTS

*Windmills*  8
*Half Hitch*  11
*Sunday Best*  14
*Magnolia Bay Gazette*  18
*Woodruff*  21
*Velocity*  24
*Cheers!*  28
*Lattice Stars*  32
*Pinwheels Plus*  36
*Tiles*  39
*Nanny's Garden*  43
*Candy Bracelet*  47
*Off Course*  51
*Gypsy*  54
*Touch a Star*  58
*Simplicity*  62
*Aviary*  65
*Wildflowers*  68

TOOLS AND SUPPLIES  75
BASIC QUILTMAKING INSTRUCTIONS  76
RESOURCES  79
ACKNOWLEDGMENTS  80
ABOUT THE AUTHOR  80

# INTRODUCTION

**The first time I saw a precut bundle of 2½"-wide strips, I thought the person who decided to package 40 little pieces of fabric, one of each print in the collection, was an absolute genius.** I still do. What's not to love about beautifully coordinated bundles of fabrics, precut and ready to use? Not only do they contain scrumptious pieces of many different coordinating prints or solids, they make the cutting part of the quilting process a breeze. There's no need to unfold, iron, and refold fabric. Just open the precut package and get started. If you haven't developed a lot of confidence when it comes to selecting fabrics that work well together in a quilt, good news! The fabric designer has already done that for you!

Some of the quilts in this book can be made with almost any precut collection of fabrics. Others were designed to use specific collections or were made with scraps and stash fabrics cut into 5" and 10" squares and 2½"-wide strips. By the time this book is released, most of the fabric collections used for the sample quilts will have been discontinued. Fortunately, a lot of our favorite fabric designers will create new collections in their unique style, using new prints and colors. If you'd like to create the look of one of my quilts, determine what about it appeals to you. Is it the fabric pattern, the fabric color, or the design of the quilt? If it's the fabric collection, look for similar collections using the same range in value (light and dark). If it's the color, you'll be able to easily collect fabrics that represent the colors in the quilt. If it's the quilt design, your possibilities are endless. You can use whatever fabrics you like to make your quilt reflect your own style.

Some of the quilts use fewer pieces than you might have in your precut bundle. You can set aside the extra pieces for future projects, or make additional blocks to make your quilt larger. Other quilts, especially those made with scraps or stash fabrics, may require more pieces than the number in your bundle. If you're using a precut collection of fabrics, just purchase a few extra pieces of matching yardage or fat quarters and scatter those prints throughout the quilt.

As much as I love precut bundles, I know there are quilters who prefer to use a wider range of fabrics for their projects instead of just one collection. My hope is that you find quilts here that you'll enjoy making whether you're a lover of precuts or someone who prefers to coordinate your own fabrics. Just have fun!

# THINGS TO KNOW ABOUT PRECUTS

**Precut fabrics come in a variety of shapes and sizes, but this book contains designs using 5" and 10" squares and 2½"-wide strips.** These are all popular precut sizes and you can find them in almost every quilt shop in many different styles and colors, including solids. Precut collections usually contain at least one piece, sometimes two, of every fabric in a collection. Bundles offered by different manufacturers vary in the number of pieces. Many bundles contain 40 or 42 pieces; others may have fewer pieces. So check the packaging to make sure you have a sufficient number of pieces to make the pattern.

Here are a few more things to note when working with precuts.

## PREWASHING

If you're thinking about prewashing your precut fabrics, just don't. It's messy. And by messy, I mean you'll end up with weird-shaped pieces of fabric with frayed edges and wrinkles. When I started quilting, most of the quilting books I read recommended prewashing fabrics. I would never have considered using unwashed fabrics in my quilts. I'm not a fabric expert by anyone's definition, but it seems that quality fabrics these days are much more colorfast and reliable. Besides, I'd rather spend time sewing and quilting than washing and ironing fabric. If you're worried about colors bleeding onto other fabrics when you launder your quilt, use cold water with gentle soap, and try using a Color Catcher product that absorbs loose dyes. Use a cool setting on your dryer to prevent fading.

## PINKED EDGES

The first time I purchased a precut bundle of strips, I was a little baffled by the pinked edges along the length of the strip. If you've never sewn with precuts, you may find these zigzagged edges a little worrisome. But there's really nothing to it. If you're sewing a pinked edge of precut fabric to a straight edge of another fabric, align the *outermost* point of the precut fabric with the straight edge of the other fabric. Sew ¼" from the edge.

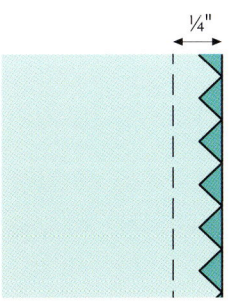

When sewing together two precut fabrics that both have pinked edges, align the outermost points of the edges as closely as possible, then sew using a ¼" seam allowance by aligning the outer points with the ¼" seam gauge on your machine, or with the edge of the ¼" presser foot.

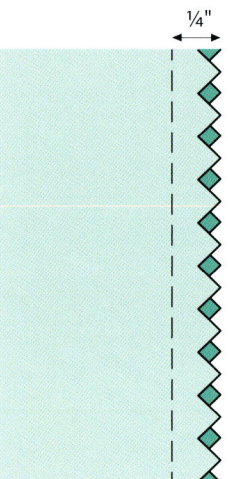

## MEASURE

Purchase precut bundles that are produced by reputable manufacturers, and *always* measure the precut fabrics before cutting pieces for your project. I've purchased bundles that included pieces that were cut smaller (or larger) than the measurements stated on the package. My intention is not to disparage any fabric manufacturers, but to warn you that there's a chance your precuts may not be exactly the right size, resulting in issues with the accuracy of your piecing. For instance, I once purchased a bundle of precut 2½"-wide strips that ranged from 2¾" wide to 2⅛" wide. All in the same strip! I trimmed the too-large section to the correct width, but the smaller sections ended up in my scrap basket. If you remember to measure before beginning your project, you'll avoid issues that may arise from using incorrectly cut pieces.

## SHRINKAGE

Fabric shrinks. It just does. It's not a bad thing, but it happens. When using precut fabrics, especially squares, I like to quickly press the individual pieces, using a little steam, and sometimes the steam can shrink fabric that hasn't yet been washed.

For the quilts in this book that use precut 5" or 10" squares, I purposely used cutting dimensions that would result in a little extra fabric in each square so that if you like to press before cutting, you'll still be able to cut the required number of pieces from your squares. For example, you may need to trim 5" squares to 4½" x 4½" for your quilt blocks. For the projects that call for scraps or stash fabrics, I've sometimes used a full 5" or 10" square since I press my stash fabrics and scraps with steam before cutting.

## FABRIC SWAPS

The quilts in this book are perfect candidates for fabric swaps. Just choose a project and host a precut swap. Look for participants at your quilt guild and on social media platforms such as Facebook and Instagram. The swap guidelines can vary, but should at least require that all fabrics are good-quality quilting fabrics. Ask each participant to contribute a predetermined number of cut pieces to swap with others. Make sure that participants are aware of and understand the swap guidelines, including deadlines for submitting their swap fabrics. If you're hosting a swap through social media, you'll need to allow time for participants to mail their swap fabrics.

# SPECIAL PIECING TECHNIQUES

Triangle-free piecing techniques are used throughout this book to create triangles and trapezoid shapes from only squares and rectangles.

## FOLDED-CORNER UNITS

You could use several methods to achieve the same result, but my two favorite methods for making folded-corner units are explained here.

### Marking

Using a small ruler and a mechanical pencil, draw a diagonal line from corner to corner on the wrong side of a 2½" fabric square. With right sides together and corners aligned, place a square on top of a fabric rectangle for folded-corner units (or on top of another square for half-square-triangle units) and sew on the drawn line. Fold up the square and match the corners and edges to make sure you've sewn accurately. If your corners don't meet, you may need to sew the seam again, stitching closer to the upper corner by a thread width or two. If the corners meet, press the triangle in place. Fold the triangle back down and trim the excess fabric, leaving ¼" seam allowances. Press back into place.

### No Marking

If you don't enjoy marking the diagonal lines on your folded corners, you can use a temporary seam guide. Cut a piece of painter's tape about 3½" to 4" long. Place the tape on the bed of your sewing machine, lining up one long edge with the needle and making sure the tape doesn't touch the feed dogs. Place the point of the unit to be sewn directly in front of the needle and make sure the other point is lined up with the edge of the painter's tape. Sew the unit, guiding the opposite point along the edge of the tape until it reaches the needle.

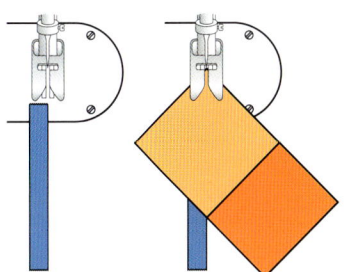

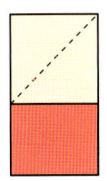
Sew on the diagonal line.

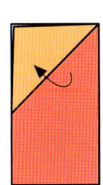
Check accuracy.

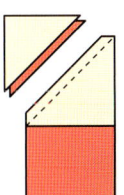
Trim seam allowances.

Press back into place.

# Windmills

*This interlocking design may look tricky, but it's actually quite easy to piece. Just be sure to arrange the rectangle units before you begin sewing them into blocks. Once you have a plan, sewing the units into blocks will be a breeze.*

## MATERIALS

Yardage is based on 42"-wide fabric.

25 matching pairs (50 total) of squares, 5" x 5", in assorted medium to dark prints for blocks
1¼ yards of white solid for blocks, border, and binding
1⅓ yards of fabric for backing
39" x 39" piece of batting

## CUTTING FROM PRECUTS AND YARDAGE

**From *each* of the assorted print squares, cut:**
2 rectangles, 2½" x 4½" (100 total)

**From the white solid, cut:**
8 strips, 2½" x 42"; crosscut *4 of the strips* into 28 rectangles, 2½" x 4½". (Set aside the remaining 2½" x 42" strips for binding.)
12 strips, 1½" x 42"; crosscut *8 of the strips* into 200 squares, 1½" x 1½". (Set aside the remaining 1½" x 42" strips for the border.)

## CUTTING FROM SCRAPS

*If you prefer to use scraps instead of precuts, follow the instructions below. See "Cutting from Precuts and Yardage" at left for instructions on cutting the border and binding.*

**From assorted medium to dark prints, cut:**
25 matching sets of 4 rectangles, 2½" x 4½" (100 total)

**From assorted light prints, cut:**
28 rectangles, 2½" x 4½"
200 squares, 1½" x 1½"

*"Windmills," pieced and quilted by Kim Brackett*

**FINISHED QUILT: 34½" x 34½"  ▪  FINISHED BLOCK: 4" x 4"**

## BLOCK ASSEMBLY

1. Referring to "Folded-Corner Units" on page 7, make a folded-corner unit as shown, using one print rectangle and two white squares. Press the seam allowances toward the white square. Make 25 sets of four identical units (100 total).

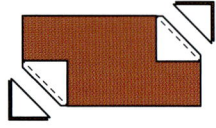 

Make 4.

2. Arrange the white rectangles and units from step 1 as shown, making sure each of the folded-corner units is oriented correctly. The four identical units should form a "pinwheel" design.

Block layout

3. Sew white rectangles and folded-corner units together to make the edge blocks. Press the seam allowances toward the white rectangle.

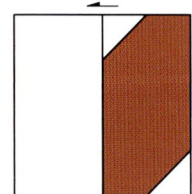

4. Sew the folded-corner units together in pairs to make the center blocks. Press the seam allowances in either direction.

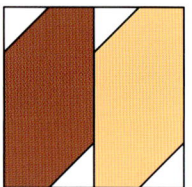

## QUILT ASSEMBLY AND FINISHING

For help with any of the finishing steps, go to ShopMartingale.com/HowtoQuilt for free, downloadable instructions.

1. Arrange the blocks in eight horizontal rows of eight blocks each as shown, making sure the identical units form a pinwheel design. Sew the blocks together in rows, pressing the seam allowances as shown. Join the rows. Press the seam allowances in one direction.

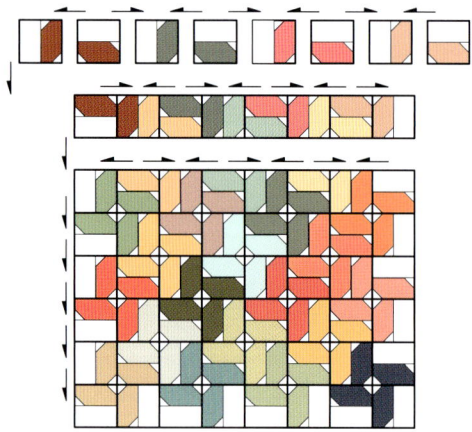

Quilt assembly

2. Referring to "Butted-Corner Borders" on page 76, add the white 1½"-wide strips for the border.
3. Layer the quilt top, batting, and backing; baste the layers together. Quilt as desired.
4. Using the white 2½"-wide strips, bind the edges of the quilt.
5. Add a label.

# Half Hitch

*Choose a pack of 5" charm squares of your favorite collection, add a contrasting background, throw in some interesting border and binding prints, and you'll have this little quilt finished in a snap.*

## MATERIALS

*Yardage is based on 42"-wide fabric.*

32 squares, 5" x 5", of assorted red, navy, aqua, and cream prints for blocks
⅔ yard of aqua solid for blocks, inner border, and sashing
⅝ yard of multicolored stripe for middle border and binding
⅝ yard of light print for outer border
3¼ yards of fabric for backing
47" x 47" piece of batting

## CUTTING FROM PRECUTS AND YARDAGE

**From *each* of the assorted print squares, cut:**
2 strips, 2½" x 5"; crosscut *each strip* into:
    1 rectangle, 2½" x 3½" (64 total)
    1 rectangle, 1½" x 2½" (64 total)

**From the aqua solid, cut:**
8 strips, 2" x 42"; crosscut *2 of the strips* into:
    12 strips, 2" x 6½"
3 strips, 1½" x 42"; crosscut into 64 squares, 1½" x 1½"

**From the multicolored stripe, cut:**
4 strips, 1½" x 42"
5 strips, 2½" x 42"

**From the light print, cut:**
4 strips, 4½" x 42"

## CUTTING FROM SCRAPS

*If you prefer to use scraps instead of precuts, follow the instructions below. See "Cutting from Precuts and Yardage" at left for instructions on cutting the borders, sashing, and binding.*

**From assorted medium to dark prints, cut *64 matching sets* of:**
1 rectangle, 2½" x 3½"
1 rectangle, 1½" x 2½"

**From assorted background prints, cut *16 matching sets* of:**
4 squares, 1½" x 1½"

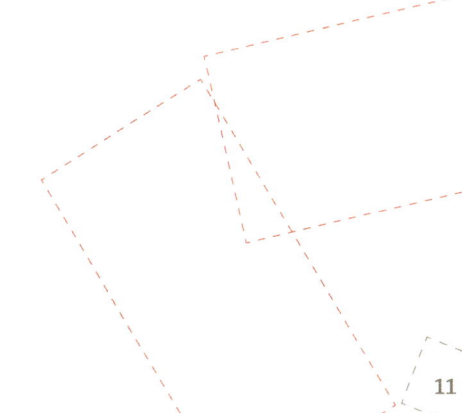

*"Half Hitch,"* pieced and quilted by Kim Brackett

**FINISHED QUILT: 42" x 42"** ▪ **FINISHED BLOCK: 6" x 6"**

## BLOCK ASSEMBLY

For each block, select four contrasting sets of print 2½" x 3½" and 1½" x 2½" rectangles.

1. Sew an aqua square to the end of a print 1½" x 2½" rectangle as shown. Press the seam allowances toward the aqua square. Make four different units.

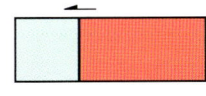

Make 4.

2. Arrange the units from step 1 and matching 2½" x 3½" rectangles as shown to resemble woven strips. Join the units and rectangles. Press the seam allowances in the directions indicated. Make four units.

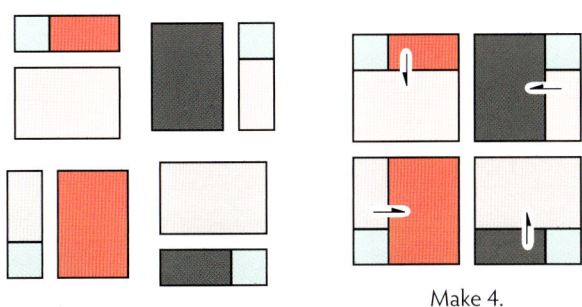

Make 4.

3. Join the units from step 2 as shown. Referring to "Pressing" on page 76, press the seam allowances in a clockwise direction. Make a total of 16 blocks.

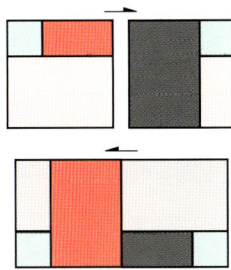 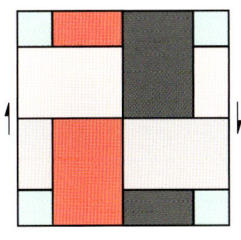

Make 16.

## QUILT ASSEMBLY AND FINISHING

For help with any of the finishing steps, go to ShopMartingale.com/HowtoQuilt for free, downloadable instructions.

1. Join the aqua 2" x 42" strips end to end. From the pieced strip, cut three 2" x 29" horizontal sashing strips. (Set aside the remainder of the pieced strip for the aqua inner border.)

2. Arrange the blocks and aqua 2" x 6½" sashing strips in four horizontal rows of four blocks each. Place the horizontal sashing strips between the rows. Sew the blocks and strips together in rows. Sew the rows and horizontal sashing strips together. Press all seam allowances toward the sashing strips.

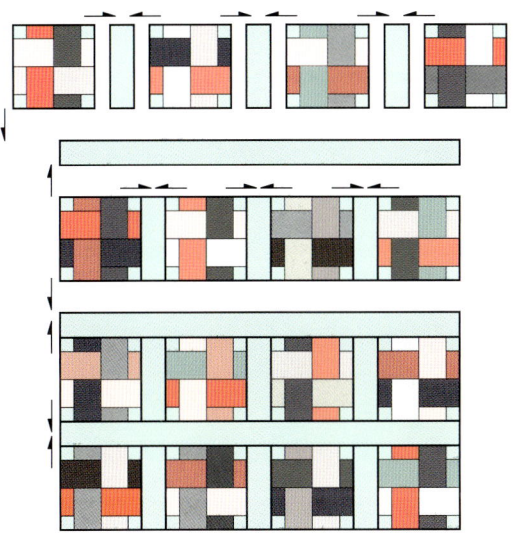

Quilt assembly

3. Referring to "Butted-Corner Borders" on page 76, add the remaining aqua 2"-wide strips from step 1 for the inner border, the multicolored-stripe 1½"-wide strips for the middle border, and the light 4½"-wide strips for the outer border.

4. Layer the quilt top, batting, and backing; baste the layers together. Quilt as desired.

5. Using the multicolored-stripe 2½"-wide strips, bind the edges of the quilt.

6. Add a label.

*Half Hitch*

# Sunday Best

The sweet prints in this fabric collection remind me of dresses my mom made for me when I was a child, but the geometric design also lends itself to more modern, or even masculine, fabrics.

## MATERIALS

*Yardage is based on 42"-wide fabric.*

27 squares, 10" x 10", of assorted light to medium prints for blocks and sashing
2 yards of navy solid for blocks and sashing
1⅓ yards of large-scale floral for outer border
1 yard of red-and-white print for inner border and binding
4½ yards of fabric for backing
69" x 81" piece of batting

## CUTTING FROM PRECUTS AND YARDAGE

**From *each* of 26 assorted light- to medium-print squares, cut:**
4 strips, 2¼" x 10". From these strips:
    Crosscut *each of 3 strips* into:
        1 rectangle, 2¼" x 5¾" (78 total)
        1 rectangle, 2¼" x 4" (78 total)
    Crosscut *1 strip* into 4 squares, 2¼" x 2¼" (104 total)

**From 1 light- to medium-print square, cut:**
4 strips, 2¼" x 10". From these strips:
    Crosscut *each of 2 strips* into:
        1 rectangle, 2¼" x 5¾" (2 total)
        1 rectangle, 2¼" x 4" (2 total)
    Crosscut *each* of the 2 remaining strips into
        4 squares, 2¼" x 2¼" (8 total; 2 are extra)

*Continued on page 16*

## CUTTING FROM SCRAPS

*If you prefer to use scraps instead of precuts, follow the instructions below. See "Cutting from Precuts and Yardage" at left for instructions on cutting the borders and binding.*

**From assorted light to medium prints, cut:**
80 matching sets of:
    1 rectangle, 2¼" x 5¾"
    1 rectangle, 2¼" x 4"
    1 square, 2¼" x 2¼"
30 squares, 2¼" x 2¼"

**From assorted dark prints, cut:**
20 matching sets of:
    4 rectangles, 2¼" x 4"
    4 squares, 2¼" x 2¼"
49 rectangles, 2¼" x 11"

*"Sunday Best,"* pieced and quilted by Kim Brackett

**FINISHED QUILT: 64¼" x 76½"** ▪ **FINISHED BLOCK: 10½" x 10½"**

*Continued from page 14*

### From the navy solid, cut:
3 strips, 11" x 42"; crosscut into 49 strips, 2¼" x 11"
5 strips, 4" x 42"; crosscut into 80 rectangles, 2¼" x 4"
5 strips, 2¼" x 42"; crosscut into 80 squares, 2¼" x 2¼"

### From the red-and-white print, cut:
6 strips, 1½" x 42"
8 strips, 2½" x 42"

### From the large-scale floral, cut:
7 strips, 6" x 42"

## BLOCK ASSEMBLY

For each block, select four matching sets of print 2¼" x 5¾" rectangles, 2¼" x 4" rectangles, and 2¼" squares.

1. Sew a print square to a navy square. Press the seam allowances in either direction. Make four different units for each block.

Make 4.

2. Sew a matching print 2¼" x 4" rectangle to the unit from step 1. Press the seam allowances toward the rectangle. Make four different units for each block.

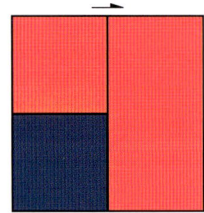

Make 4.

3. Sew a navy 2¼" x 4" rectangle to the unit from step 2 as shown. Press the seam allowances in either direction. Make four different units for each block.

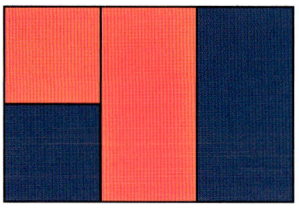

Make 4.

4. Arrange the units from step 3 and matching print 2¼" x 5¾" rectangles as shown. Sew the rectangles to each of the units to make four quadrants. Press the seam allowances toward the just-added rectangles.

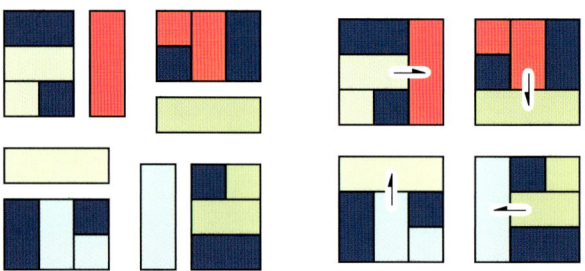

5. Sew the quadrants from step 4 together. Referring to "Pressing" on page 76, press the seam allowances in a counter-clockwise direction. Make a total of 20 blocks.

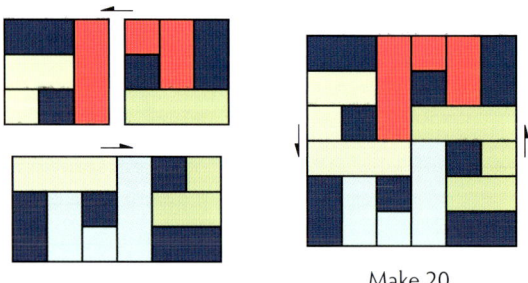

Make 20.

## QUILT ASSEMBLY AND FINISHING

For help with any of the finishing steps, go to ShopMartingale.com/HowtoQuilt for free, downloadable instructions.

1. Arrange the blocks, navy 2¼" x 11" sashing strips, and print 2¼" squares as shown. Sew the pieces together in rows, pressing the seam allowances toward the sashing strips. Sew the rows together. Press the seam allowances in one direction.

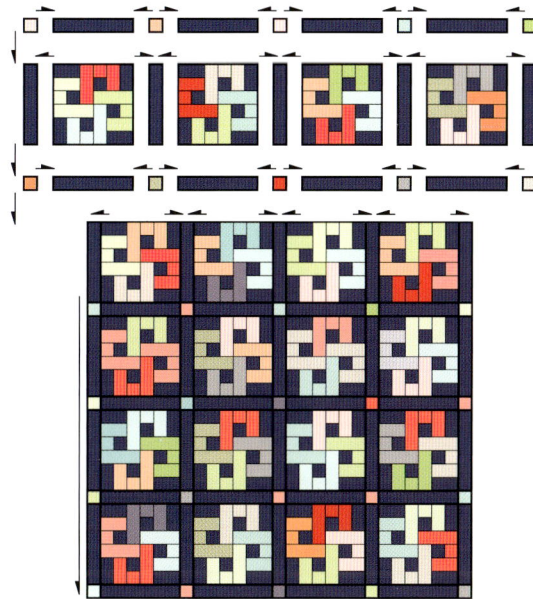

Quilt assembly

2. Referring to "Butted-Corner Borders" on page 76, add the red-and-white 1½"-wide strips for the inner border and the floral 6"-wide strips for the outer border.
3. Layer the quilt top, batting, and backing; baste the layers together. Quilt as desired.
4. Using the red-and-white 2½"-wide strips, bind the edges of the quilt.
5. Add a label.

# Magnolia Bay Gazette

It's almost impossible for me to resist buying fabrics with words, letters, or numbers. If you haven't yet developed an obsession with these fun prints and would like to re-create the look of this quilt, look for charm-square swaps on social-media platforms. Or host your own!

## MATERIALS

*Yardage is based on 42"-wide fabric.*

65 squares, 5" x 5", of assorted text prints for blocks
32 squares, 5" x 5", of assorted red prints for blocks
⅜ yard of red print for binding
1⅓ yards of fabric for backing
41" x 41" piece of batting

## CUTTING FROM PRECUTS AND YARDAGE

**From *each* of 16 red squares, cut:**
4 squares, 2½" x 2½" (64 total)

**From *each* of 16 red squares, cut:**
1 square, 4½" x 4½" (16 total)

**From *each* of 40 text-print squares, cut:**
2 rectangles, 2½" x 4½" (80 total)

**From *each* of 25 text-print squares, cut:**
1 square, 4½" x 4½" (25 total)

**From the red print, cut:**
4 strips, 2½" x 42"

## CUTTING FROM SCRAPS

If you prefer to use scraps instead of precuts, follow the instructions below. See "Cutting from Precuts and Yardage" at left for instructions on cutting the borders and binding.

**From assorted red prints, cut:**
16 squares, 4½" x 4½"
64 squares, 2½" x 2½"

**From assorted light prints, cut:**
25 squares, 4½" x 4½"
40 matching sets of 2 rectangles, 2½" x 4½" (80 total)

*"Magnolia Bay Gazette,"* pieced and quilted by Kim Brackett

**FINISHED QUILT: 36½" x 36½" ▪ FINISHED BLOCK: 4" x 4"**

## BLOCK ASSEMBLY

1. Referring to "Folded-Corner Units" on page 7, make a folded-corner unit as shown using a text-print rectangle and a red 2½" square. Press the seam allowances toward the red triangle. Make 16.

   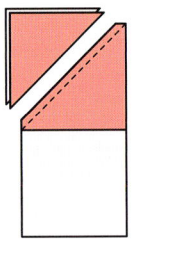 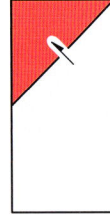

   Make 16.

2. Sew a matching text-print rectangle to a unit from step 1. Press the seam allowances toward the text-print rectangle. Make 16 blocks.

   Make 16.

3. Make two folded-corner units using two matching text-print rectangles and two *different* red 2½" squares as shown. Press the seam allowances toward the red triangles. Make 24 sets of two matching units.

   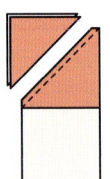  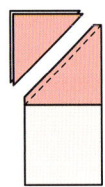 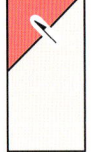

   Make 24 sets.

4. Join two matching units from step 3 as shown. Press the seam allowances in either direction. Make 24 blocks.

   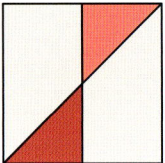

   Make 24.

## QUILT ASSEMBLY AND FINISHING

For help with any of the finishing steps, go to ShopMartingale.com/HowtoQuilt for free, downloadable instructions.

1. Arrange the blocks from steps 2 and 4 of "Block Assembly," along with the red and text-print 4½" squares as shown, placing the blocks from step 2 along the outer edges. Sew the blocks and squares together in horizontal rows, pressing the seam allowances toward the 4½" squares as indicated. Sew the rows together. Press the seam allowances in one direction.

   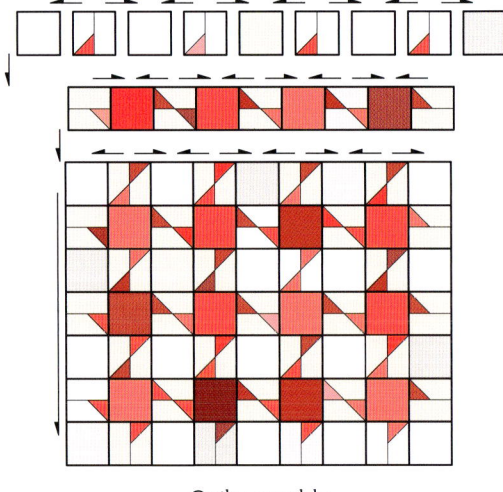

   Quilt assembly

2. Layer the quilt top, batting, and backing; baste the layers together. Quilt as desired.

3. Using the red 2½"-wide strips, bind the edges of the quilt.

4. Add a label.

*Scrap-Basket Strips and Squares*

# Woodruff

*Determined that this would be a "flower quilt," I searched for flowers with four petals to come up with a name for this quilt. I just knew there would be one that looked exactly like my quilt block! Unfortunately, I couldn't find an exact match, but the woodruff came closer than most.*

## MATERIALS

*Yardage is based on 42"-wide fabric.*

16 matching pairs (32 total) of squares, 5" x 5" in assorted dark batiks for blocks
1 yard of cream print for blocks
⅝ yard of red batik for inner border and binding
⅝ yard of multicolored batik for outer border
3¼ yards of fabric for backing
47" x 47" piece of batting

## CUTTING FROM PRECUTS AND YARDAGE

**From *each* of the assorted dark-batik squares, cut:**
2 rectangles, 2½" x 4½" (64 total)

**From the cream print, cut:**
8 strips, 2½" x 42"; crosscut into 64 rectangles, 2½" x 4½"
5 strips, 1½" x 42"; crosscut into 128 squares, 1½" x 1½"

**From the red batik, cut:**
4 strips, 1½" x 42"
5 strips, 2½" x 42"

**From the multicolored batik, cut:**
4 strips, 4½" x 42"

## CUTTING FROM SCRAPS

*If you prefer to use scraps instead of precuts, follow the instructions below. See "Cutting from Precuts and Yardage" at left for instructions on cutting the borders and binding.*

**From assorted dark prints, cut *16 matching sets* of:**
4 rectangles, 2½" x 4½"

**From assorted light prints, cut *16 matching sets* of:**
4 rectangles, 2½" x 4½"
8 squares, 1½" x 1½"

*"Woodruff," pieced and quilted by Kim Brackett*

**FINISHED QUILT: 42½" x 42½"  ▪  FINISHED BLOCK: 8" x 8"**

## BLOCK ASSEMBLY

1. Referring to "Folded-Corner Units" on page 7, make folded-corner units as shown, using a dark-batik rectangle and two cream squares. Press the seam allowances toward the cream triangles. Make four identical units for each block.

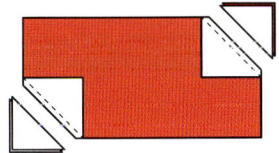 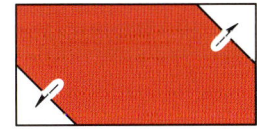

Make 4.

2. Sew a cream rectangle to each unit from step 1. Press the seam allowances toward the cream rectangle. Make four identical units for each block.

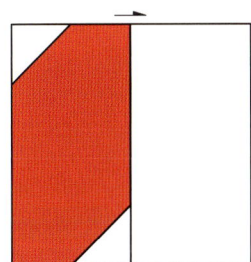

Make 4.

3. Sew the units from step 2 together as shown. Referring to "Pressing" on page 76, press the seam allowances in a clockwise direction. Make a total of 16 blocks.

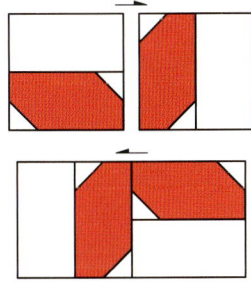 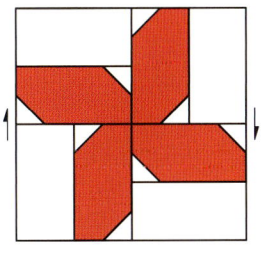

Make 16.

## QUILT ASSEMBLY AND FINISHING

For help with any of the finishing steps, go to ShopMartingale.com/HowtoQuilt for free, downloadable instructions.

1. Arrange the blocks in four horizontal rows of four blocks each as shown. Sew the blocks together in rows, pressing the seam allowances in alternating directions from row to row. Join the rows. Press the seam allowances in one direction.

Quilt assembly

2. Referring to "Butted-Corner Borders" on page 76, add the red-batik 1½"-wide strips for the inner border and the multicolored-batik strips for the outer border.

3. Layer the quilt top, batting, and backing; baste the layers together. Quilt as desired.

4. Using the red-batik 2½"-wide strips, bind the edges of the quilt.

5. Add a label.

*Woodruff*

# Velocity

*This quilt is not nearly as complicated as it looks. Take the time to arrange your fabrics before you start sewing blocks, and you won't have any trouble figuring out which piece goes next to another. Not one for planning ahead? You can always take it a block at a time.*

## MATERIALS

*Yardage is based on 42"-wide fabric.*

36 squares, 10" x 10", of assorted medium to dark prints for blocks
1⅜ yards of gray solid for blocks
1⅛ yards of gray-and-yellow print for outer border
⅞ yard of yellow print for inner border and binding
4¼ yards of fabric for backing
66" x 74" piece of batting

## CUTTING FROM PRECUTS AND YARDAGE

**From the gray solid, cut:**
3 strips, 5" x 42"; crosscut into 24 squares, 5" x 5". Cut each square in half diagonally to yield 48 triangles.
11 strips, 2½" x 42"; crosscut into 168 squares, 2½" x 2½"

**From the yellow print, cut:**
6 strips, 1½" x 42"
7 strips, 2½" x 42"

**From the gray-and-yellow print, cut:**
6 strips, 6" x 42"

## CUTTING FROM SCRAPS

*If you prefer to use scraps instead of precuts, follow the instructions below. See "Cutting from Precuts and Yardage" at left for instructions on cutting the borders and binding.*

**From assorted medium to dark prints, cut:**
72 matching sets of 2 squares, 5" x 5"; cut the squares in half diagonally to yield 288 triangles.

*"Velocity," pieced and quilted by Kim Brackett*

**FINISHED QUILT: 61½" x 69½"  ▪  FINISHED BLOCK: 4" x 4"**

## BLOCK ASSEMBLY

This quilt requires a little planning before assembling the blocks. If you begin sewing the blocks willy-nilly, there's a chance you'll spend more time ripping seams than sewing them. Ask me how I know!

1. Cut each of the print squares in half horizontally and vertically. Without disturbing the placement of the fabric, cut the squares in half diagonally as shown to yield eight triangles.

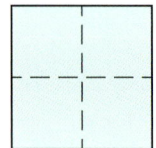 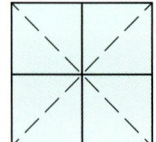

One 10" square yields 8 triangles.

2. Lay out the print triangles as shown in the block layout at right, placing four matching triangles together to form a big on-point square. Place the gray triangles around the edges. Try to place contrasting fabrics next to each other to maximize the design. Once you have all the triangles laid out in a pleasing arrangement, it's a good idea to snap a picture in case your fabric arrangement is disturbed or you have to move the pieces before they're sewn together.

3. Sew the triangles together along their long sides to make half-square-triangle units. Trim each unit to 4½" x 4½". Double-check the layout to make sure you've sewn the triangles correctly, and the seams are positioned correctly.

Block layout

4. Referring to "Folded-Corner Units" on page 7, sew a gray square to each half-square-triangle unit as shown to make a block. Pay careful attention to the placement of the gray square on each block. You may find it helpful to pin a gray square on each block on the corner where the square will be stitched. The illustration below shows a few blocks from the first two rows. Press the seam allowances toward the gray triangle. Make a total of 168 blocks.

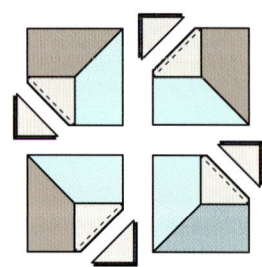 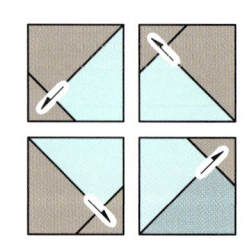

Make 168.

*Scrap-Basket Strips and Squares*

## QUILT ASSEMBLY AND FINISHING

For help with any of the finishing steps, go to ShopMartingale.com/HowtoQuilt for free, downloadable instructions.

1. Arrange the blocks in 14 horizontal rows of 12 blocks each as shown. Sew the blocks together in rows, pressing the seam allowances in alternating directions from row to row. Join the rows. Press the seam allowances in one direction.

Quilt assembly

2. Referring to "Butted-Corner Borders" on page 76, add the yellow 1½"-wide strips for the inner border and the gray-and-yellow 6"-wide strips for the outer border.

3. Layer the quilt top, batting, and backing; baste the layers together. Quilt as desired.

4. Using the yellow 2½"-wide strips, bind the edges of the quilt.

5. Add a label.

# Cheers!

*When I designed this quilt block, I thought it looked like wine glasses, thus the name, "Cheers!" I've since been told it also looks like half a piece of wrapped candy and a headless fish. Whatever you see, I think you'll have fun piecing this quilt.*

## MATERIALS

*Yardage is based on 42"-wide fabric.*

49 matching pairs (98 total) of squares, 5" x 5", in assorted dark prints for blocks and outer border

49 matching pairs (98 total) of squares, 5" x 5", in assorted light prints for blocks

12 squares, 5" x 5", of assorted dark prints for outer border

¾ yard of turquoise print for inner border and binding

3¾ yards of fabric for backing

57" x 57" piece of batting

## CUTTING FROM PRECUTS AND YARDAGE

**From *each* of the 49 matching pairs of assorted dark-print squares, cut:**
1 square, 4½" x 4½" (49 total)
4 squares, 2½" x 2½" (196 total)

**From *each* of the 12 assorted dark-print squares, cut:**
4 squares, 2½" x 2½" (48 total; 3 are extra)

**From *each* of the 49 matching pairs of assorted light-print squares, cut:**
2 rectangles, 2½" x 4½" (98 total)
4 squares, 2½" x 2½" (196 total)

**From the turquoise print, cut:**
5 strips, 1½" x 42"
6 strips, 2½" x 42"

## CUTTING FROM SCRAPS

*If you prefer to use scraps instead of precuts, follow the instructions below. See "Cutting from Precuts and Yardage" at left for instructions on cutting the borders and binding.*

### BLOCKS:

**From assorted dark prints, cut *49 matching sets* of:**
1 square, 4½" x 4½"
1 square, 2½" x 2½"

**From assorted light prints, cut *49 matching sets* of:**
2 rectangles, 2½" x 4½"
4 squares, 2½" x 2½"

### PIECED BORDER:

**From assorted dark prints, cut:**
192 squares, 2½" x 2½"

*"Cheers!" pieced and quilted by Kim Brackett*

**FINISHED QUILT: 52½" x 52½"** ▪ **FINISHED BLOCK: 6" x 6"**

## BLOCK ASSEMBLY

For each block, you'll need a dark 4½" square and a dark 2½" square from the same print. You'll also need four light squares and two rectangles, all matching.

1. Referring to "Folded Corner Units" on page 7, sew two matching light squares to opposite corners of a dark 4½" square as shown. Press the seam allowances toward the light triangles. Make one for each block.

   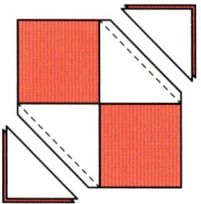 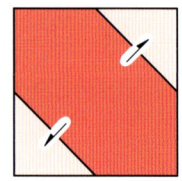
   Make 1.

2. Sew a matching light square to the unit from step 1 as shown to complete the folded-corner unit. Press the seam allowances toward the light triangle. Make one for each block.

   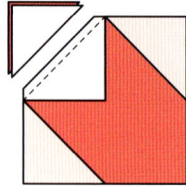 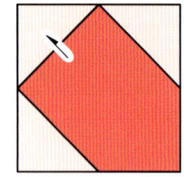
   Make 1.

3. Sew a matching light rectangle to the unit from step 2 as shown. Press the seam allowances toward the light rectangle. Make one for each block.

   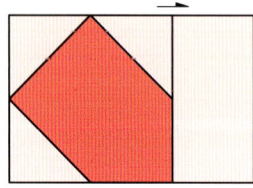
   Make 1.

4. Referring to "Folded-Corner Units," make a half-square-triangle unit using a light square and a dark 2½" square. Press the seam allowances toward the dark triangle. Make one for each block.

    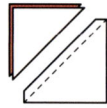 
   Make 1.

5. Sew a matching light rectangle to the half-square-triangle unit from step 4. Press the seam allowances toward the light rectangle. Make one for each block.

   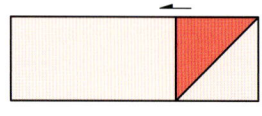
   Make 1.

6. Sew the unit from step 5 to the unit from step 3 as shown. Press the seam allowances in the direction indicated. Make a total of 49 blocks.

   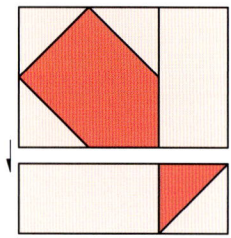 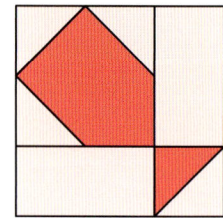
   Make 49.

## PIECED BORDER ASSEMBLY

Using the remaining dark 2½" squares, assemble four-patch units for the pieced border as shown. Referring to "Pressing" on page 76, press the seam allowances in a clockwise direction. Make 48 four-patch units.

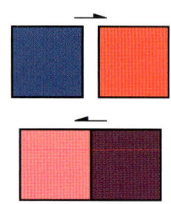 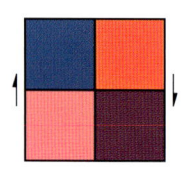
Make 48.

*Scrap-Basket Strips and Squares*

## QUILT ASSEMBLY AND FINISHING

For help with any of the finishing steps, go to ShopMartingale.com/HowtoQuilt for free, downloadable instructions.

1. Arrange the blocks in seven horizontal rows of seven blocks each, rotating every other block as shown. Sew the blocks together in rows, pressing the seam allowances in alternating directions from row to row. Join the rows. Press the seam allowances in one direction.

Quilt assembly

2. Join the turquoise 1½"-wide strips end to end. From the pieced strip, cut two 44½"-long strips and two 42½"-long strips.

3. Sew the turquoise 42½"-long strips to the sides of the quilt top. Press the seam allowances toward the strips. Sew the turquoise 44½"-long strips to the top and bottom of the quilt top to complete the inner border. Press the seam allowances toward the inner-border strips.

4. Join 11 four-patch units for each of the side borders. Join 13 four-patch units for each of the top and bottom borders. Press the seam allowances in either direction.

5. Sew the pieced borders to the sides of the quilt top first, and then add the top and bottom borders. Press the seam allowances toward the inner border.

Adding borders

6. Layer the quilt top, batting, and backing; baste the layers together. Quilt as desired.

7. Using the turquoise 2½"-wide strips, bind the edges of the quilt.

8. Add a label.

*Cheers!* 31

# Lattice Stars

This quilt is a great way to use all of your small scraps. Select contrasting light and dark prints to make your quilt sparkle.

### MATERIALS

Yardage is based on 42"-wide fabric.

208 squares, 5" x 5", of assorted dark prints for blocks*
144 squares, 5" x 5", of assorted light prints for blocks
⅝ yard of gray print for binding
4½ yards of fabric for backing
69" x 69" piece of batting

*See note in "Cutting from Precuts and Yardage" below if you're using scraps or stash fabrics.

### CUTTING FROM PRECUTS AND YARDAGE

The cutting measurements assume you're using precut 5" x 5" squares. If you're using scraps or stash fabrics, follow the cutting directions in the "Cutting from Scraps" box, and you won't need to trim the 5" squares down to a useable size.

**From *each* of 192 assorted dark-print squares, cut:**
1 square, 4½" x 4½" (192 total)

**From *each* of 16 assorted dark-print squares, cut:**
2 strips, 2½" x 5"; crosscut into 4 squares, 2½" x 2½" (64 total)

**From *each* of 80 light-print squares, cut:**
2 strips, 2½" x 5"; crosscut into 4 squares, 2½" x 2½" (320 total)

**From *each* of 64 light-print squares, cut:**
1 square, 4½" x 4½" (64 total)

**From the gray print, cut:**
7 strips, 2½" x 42"

### CUTTING FROM SCRAPS

If you prefer to use scraps instead of precuts, follow the instructions below. See "Cutting from Precuts and Yardage" at left for instructions on cutting the borders and binding.

**From assorted dark prints, cut:**
192 squares, 4½" x 4½"
64 squares, 2½" x 2½"

**From assorted light prints, cut:**
64 squares, 4½" x 4½"
320 squares, 2½" x 2½"

"Lattice Stars," pieced and quilted by Kim Brackett

**FINISHED QUILT: 64½" x 64½" ▪ FINISHED BLOCK: 16" x 16"**

## BLOCK ASSEMBLY

1. Referring to "Folded-Corner Units" on page 7, make a folded-corner unit as shown, using a dark 4½" square and a light 2½" square. Press the seam allowances toward the light triangle. Make four units for each block.

   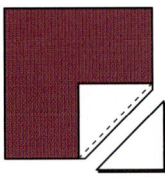 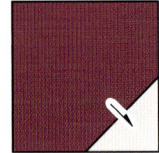

   Make 4.

2. Make a folded-corner unit using a light 4½" square and a dark 2½" square. Press the seam allowances toward the dark triangle. Make four units for each block.

   Make 4.

3. Make a folded-corner unit using a dark 4½" square and two light 2½" squares as shown. Press the seam allowances toward the light triangles. Make eight units for each block.

   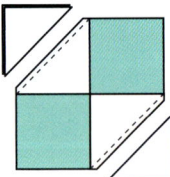 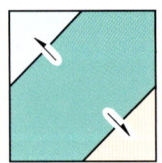

   Make 8.

4. Sew the units from steps 1, 2, and 3 together as shown to make a quadrant. Referring to "Pressing" on page 76, press the seam allowances in a counter-clockwise direction. Make four for each block.

   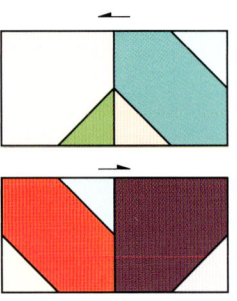 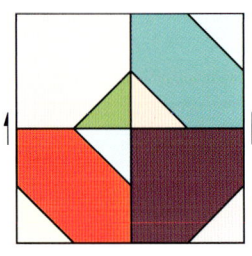

   Make 4.

5. Sew the quadrants from step 4 together as shown to make a block. Press the seam allowances in a counter-clockwise direction. Make a total of 16 blocks.

   Make 16.

*Scrap-Basket Strips and Squares*

## QUILT ASSEMBLY AND FINISHING

For help with any of the finishing steps, go to ShopMartingale.com/HowtoQuilt for free, downloadable instructions.

1. Arrange the blocks in four horizontal rows of four blocks each. Sew the blocks together in rows, pressing the seam allowances in alternating directions from row to row. Join the rows. Press the seam allowances in one direction.

Quilt assembly

2. Layer the quilt top, batting, and backing; baste the layers together. Quilt as desired.
3. Using the gray-print 2½"-wide strips, bind the edges of the quilt.
4. Add a label.

# Pinwheels Plus

*Bright, contemporary fabrics lend a modern quality to this pattern. Using the same background fabric for the border makes the blocks appear to float on the quilt. For a more traditional look, use reproduction fabrics for the blocks and a print fabric for the border.*

## MATERIALS

*Yardage is based on 42"-wide fabric.*

30 squares, 10" x 10", of assorted light, medium, and dark prints for blocks
3⅝ yards of charcoal solid for blocks, border, and binding
4 yards of fabric for backing
60" x 72" piece of batting

## CUTTING FROM PRECUTS AND YARDAGE

**From *each* of 20 assorted print squares, cut:**
2 strips, 4½" x 10"; crosscut into 4 squares, 4½" x 4½" (80 total)

**From *each* of 10 assorted print squares, cut:**
4 strips, 2½" x 10"; crosscut into 8 rectangles, 2½" x 4½" (80 total)

**From the charcoal solid, cut:**
31 strips, 2½" x 42"; crosscut 24 of the strips into:
    80 rectangles, 2½" x 6½"
    160 squares, 2½" x 2½"
    (Set aside the remaining 7 strips for the binding.)
8 strips, 4½" x 42"

### CUTTING FROM SCRAPS

*If you prefer to use scraps instead of precuts, follow the instructions below. See "Cutting from Precuts and Yardage" at left for instructions on cutting the borders and binding.*

**From assorted main prints, cut *20 matching sets* of:**
4 squares, 4¼" x 4½"
4 rectangles, 2½" x 4½"

**From assorted background prints, cut *20 matching sets* of:**
4 rectangles, 2½" x 6½"
8 squares, 2½" x 2½"

"Pinwheels Plus," pieced and quilted by Karen Williamson

FINISHED QUILT: 56½" x 68½" ▪ FINISHED BLOCK: 12" x 12"

## BLOCK ASSEMBLY

1. Referring to "Folded-Corner Units" on page 7, make a folded-corner unit as shown, using a print square and two charcoal squares. Press the seam allowances toward the charcoal triangles. Make four identical units for each block.

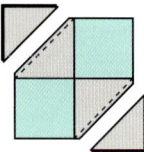

Make 4.

2. Sew a print rectangle to each unit from step 1. Press the seam allowances toward the rectangle. Make four identical units for each block.

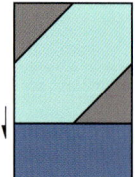

Make 4.

3. Sew a charcoal rectangle to each unit from step 2 as shown. Press the seam allowances toward the charcoal rectangle. Make four identical units for each block.

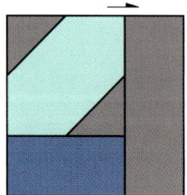

Make 4.

4. Sew the four units from step 3 together as shown above right. Referring to "Pressing" on page 76, press the seam allowances counterclockwise. Make a total of 20 blocks.

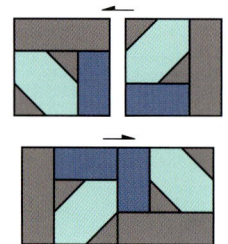 

Make 20.

## QUILT ASSEMBLY AND FINISHING

For help with any of the finishing steps, go to ShopMartingale.com/HowtoQuilt for free, downloadable instructions.

1. Arrange the blocks in five horizontal rows of four blocks each as shown. Sew the blocks together in rows, pressing the seam allowances in alternating directions from row to row. Join the rows. Press the seam allowances in one direction.

Quilt assembly

2. Referring to "Mitered-Corner Borders" on page 77, add the charcoal 4½"-wide strips for the border.
3. Layer the quilt top, batting, and backing; baste the layers together. Quilt as desired.
4. Using the charcoal 2½"-wide strips, bind the edges of the quilt.
5. Add a label.

*Scrap-Basket Strips and Squares*

# Tiles

The beauty of the Tile blocks is achieved by using partial seams during assembly. If you've never pieced a block with partial seams, you'll be happy to know they're quite easy. And you can see the results are stunning!

## MATERIALS

*Yardage is based on 42"-wide fabric.*

30 squares, 10" x 10", of assorted red, pink, orange, yellow, green, and aqua prints for blocks

1⅞ yards of white solid for blocks

⅝ yard of pink stripe for binding

4 yards of fabric for backing

59" x 69" piece of batting

## CUTTING FROM PRECUTS AND YARDAGE

**From *each* of the assorted print squares, cut:**

1 strip, 6½" x 10"; crosscut into 3 rectangles, 3" x 6½" (90 total)

1 strip, 3" x 10"; crosscut into:
　　1 rectangle, 3" x 6½" (30 total)
　　1 square, 3" x 3" (30 total)

**From the white solid, cut:**

1 strip, 10" x 42"; crosscut into 24 strips, 1½" x 10"

33 strips, 1½" x 42"

**From the pink stripe, cut:**

7 strips, 2½" x 42"

## CUTTING FROM SCRAPS

If you prefer to use scraps instead of precuts, follow the instructions below. See "Cutting from Precuts and Yardage" at left for instructions on cutting the borders and binding.

**From assorted prints, cut:**

120 rectangles, 3" x 6½"

30 squares, 3" x 3"

"Tiles," pieced and quilted by Kim Brackett

**FINISHED QUILT: 54" x 64½"** ▪ **FINISHED BLOCK: 9½" x 9½"**

## BLOCK ASSEMBLY

1. Sew the long edges of six print rectangles to a white 42"-long strip, carefully placing the print rectangles end to end. Do not overlap the rectangles. Make 20 strip sets.

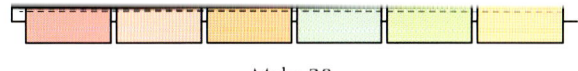

Make 20.

2. Carefully cut each strip set into six 6½" strip-pieced units as shown. Press the seam allowances toward the white strip. Make a total of 120 units.

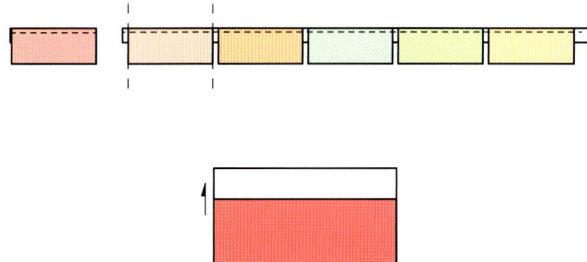

Make 120.

3. Using a partial seam, sew a print square to a unit from step 2, starting at the outer edge and stopping about halfway across the square with a backstitch. Press the seam allowances away from the center square. Make 30 units.

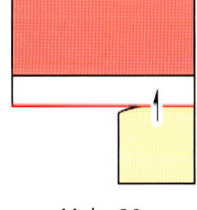

Make 30.

4. Sew three more units to the center square in the order shown. Press the seam allowances away from the center square. After the last unit is attached, complete the partial seam to make a block. Press all seam allowances away from the center square. Make a total of 30 blocks.

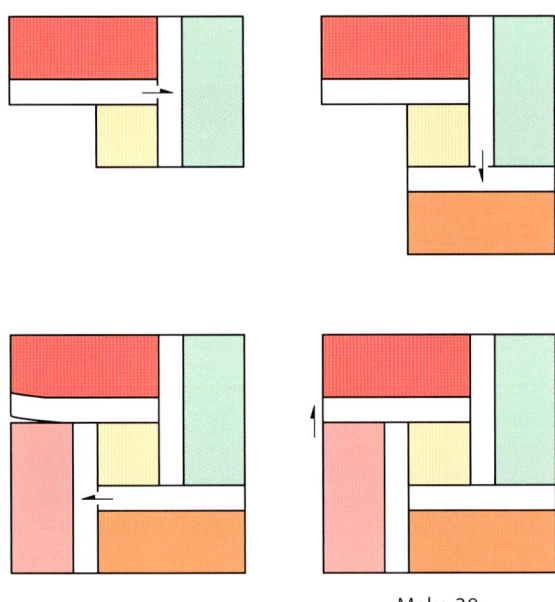

Make 30.

## QUILT ASSEMBLY AND FINISHING

For help with any of the finishing steps, go to ShopMartingale.com/HowtoQuilt for free, downloadable instructions.

1. Join the remaining 13 white strips end to end. From the pieced strip, cut seven 52"-long horizontal sashing strips and two 64½"-long vertical border strips.

2. Arrange the blocks and white 1½" x 10" sashing strips in six horizontal rows of five blocks each. Place the 52"-long horizontal sashing strips between the block rows and along the top and bottom edges as shown in the quilt assembly diagram below. Sew the blocks and strips together in rows, pressing the seam allowances toward the sashing strips. Sew the rows and horizontal sashing strips together. Press the seam allowances toward the horizontal sashing strips. Sew the 64½"-long vertical border strips to each side of the quilt top. Press the seam allowances toward the vertical border strips.

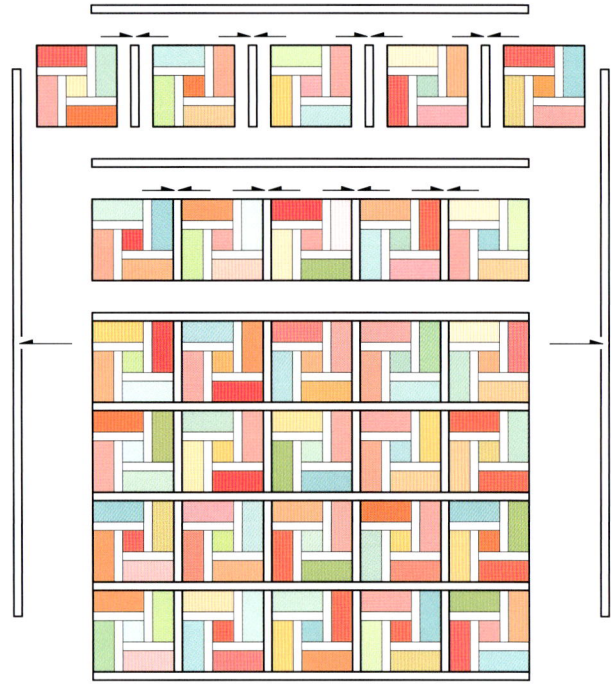

Quilt assembly

3. Layer the quilt top, batting, and backing; baste the layers together. Quilt as desired.

4. Using the pink 2½"-wide strips, bind the edges of the quilt.

5. Add a label.

*Scrap-Basket Strips and Squares*

# Nanny's Garden

*Whenever I see Depression-era reproduction fabrics, I always think of my grandmother. Working in her flower gardens brought her great joy, and she spent a lot of time digging in the dirt. Although some of these fabrics aren't actually reproductions, they work together nicely and look like fabrics that our grandmothers would have used in their quilts.*

## MATERIALS

*Yardage is based on 42"-wide fabric.*

48 squares, 10" x 10", of assorted pastel prints for blocks
1⅝ yards of white solid for blocks
⅝ yard of red print for binding
4½ yards of fabric for backing
69" x 69" piece of batting

## CUTTING FROM PRECUTS AND YARDAGE

**From the white solid, cut:**
4 strips, 10" x 42"; crosscut into 16 squares, 10" x 10"
4 strips, 2½" x 42"; crosscut into 64 squares, 2½" x 2½"

**From the red print, cut:**
7 strips, 2½" x 42"

## CUTTING FROM SCRAPS

*If you prefer to use scraps instead of precuts, follow the instructions below. See "Cutting from Precuts and Yardage" at left for instructions on cutting the borders and binding. Use 5" squares instead of 10" squares, and refer to "Folded-Corner Units" on page 7 to make 128 half-square-triangle units using one light and one dark 5" square and 128 half-square-triangle units using two dark 5" squares.*

**From assorted pastel prints, cut:**
192 squares, 5" x 5"

**From assorted light prints, cut:**
64 squares, 5" x 5"
64 squares, 2½" x 2½"

"Nanny's Garden," pieced by Kim Brackett; quilted by Karen Williamson

FINISHED QUILT: 64½" x 64½" ▪ FINISHED BLOCK: 16" X 16"

## BLOCK ASSEMBLY

1. Using a mechanical pencil or a permanent fine-tipped marker, draw intersecting diagonal lines from corner to corner on the wrong side of a white 10" square. Layer the marked square with a bright-pastel square, right sides together. Sew using a scant ¼" seam allowance along each side of both drawn lines as shown. Make 16.

   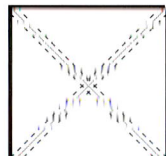

   Make 16.

2. Cut the squares apart horizontally and vertically as shown. Then cut the squares apart on the drawn diagonal lines to yield eight half-square-triangle units. Press the seam allowances *open* to avoid extra bulk when constructing the blocks. Trim each unit to measure 4½" x 4½". Repeat to make a total of 16 sets of eight identical half-square-triangle units.

   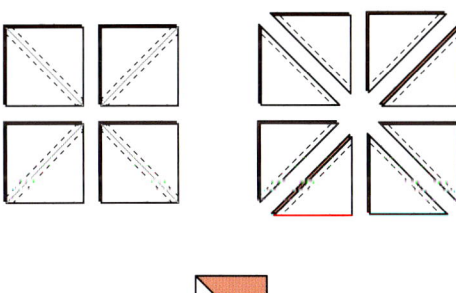

   Make 8.

3. Repeat steps 1 and 2 using two pastel squares to make eight half-square-triangle units. Make a total of 16 sets of eight half-square-triangle units.

   Make 8.

4. Select 64 units from step 3. Referring to "Folded-Corner Units" on page 7, make a folded-corner unit as shown, using a white 2½" square and a half-square-triangle unit. Press the seam allowances toward the white triangle. Make 64.

   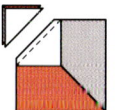 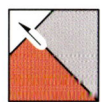

   Make 64.

5. Join two half-square-triangle units from step 2, one half-square-triangle unit from step 3, and one folded-corner unit from step 4 as shown to make a quadrant. Referring to "Pressing" on page 76, press the seam allowances in a clockwise direction. Make 64.

   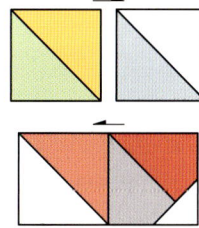 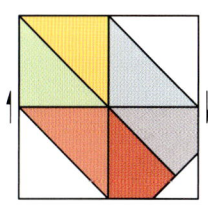

   Make 64.

6. Sew four quadrants from step 5 together as shown to make a block. Press the seam allowances in a clockwise direction. Make a total of 16 blocks.

   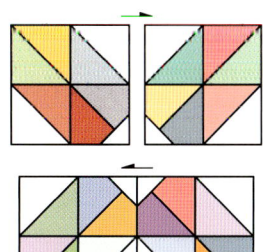 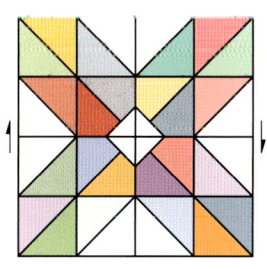

   Make 16.

*Nanny's Garden*

## QUILT ASSEMBLY AND FINISHING

For help with any of the finishing steps, go to ShopMartingale.com/HowtoQuilt for free, downloadable instructions.

1. Arrange the blocks in four horizontal rows of four blocks each as shown. Sew the blocks together in horizontal rows, pressing the seam allowances in alternating directions from row to row. Join the rows. Press the seam allowances in one direction.

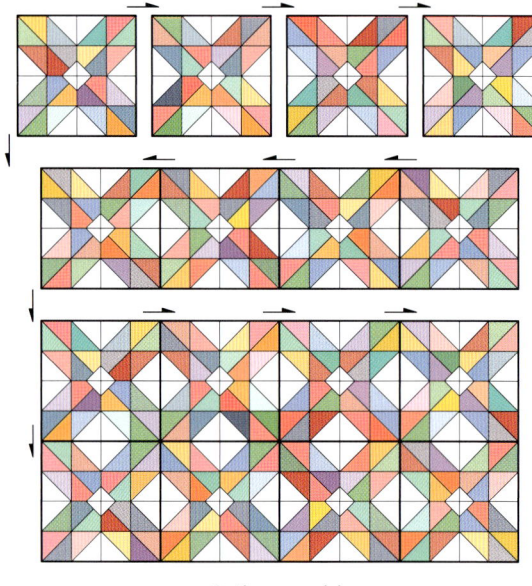

Quilt assembly

2. Layer the quilt top, batting, and backing; baste the layers together. Quilt as desired.
3. Using the red 2½"-wide strips, bind the edges of the quilt.
4. Add a label.

# Candy Bracelet

*Do you remember the candy bracelets we wore (and ate!) as children? The "beads" in my quilt are more elongated, but whenever I look at it, I can still hear my bracelet clacking.*

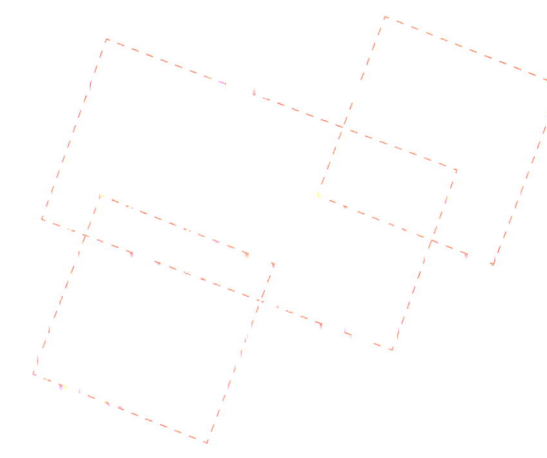

## MATERIALS

*Yardage is based on 42"-wide fabric.*

28 squares, 10" x 10", of assorted medium to dark prints in red, blue, green, pink, and yellow for blocks
2⅓ yards of white solid for blocks
1⅓ yards of blue floral for outer border
1 yard of light-green solid for blocks
⅞ yard of red-and-white print for inner border and binding
4¼ yards of fabric for backing
67" x 74" piece of batting

## CUTTING FROM PRECUTS AND YARDAGE

**From *each* of the assorted medium- to dark-print squares, cut:**
4 strips, 2¼" x 10"; crosscut *each* strip into:
    1 rectangle, 2¼" x 5¾" (112 total)
    1 rectangle, 2¼" x 4" (112 total)

**From the white solid, cut:**
4 strips, 7½" x 42"; crosscut into 112 rectangles, 1⅜" x 7½"
20 strips, 2¼" x 42"; crosscut into:
    56 rectangles, 2¼" x 4"
    224 squares, 2¼" x 2¼"

*Continued on page 49*

## CUTTING FROM SCRAPS

*If you prefer to use scraps instead of precuts, follow the instructions below. See "Cutting from Precuts and Yardage" at left for instructions on cutting the borders and binding.*

**From assorted medium to dark prints, cut 56 matching sets of:**
2 rectangles, 2¼" x 5¾"
2 rectangles, 2¼" x 4"

**From assorted light prints, cut 56 matching sets of:**
1 rectangle, 2¼" x 4"
2 rectangles, 1⅜" x 7½"
4 squares, 2¼" x 2¼"

**From assorted medium prints, cut:**
224 squares, 2⅛" x 2⅛"

"Candy Bracelet," pieced by Kim Brackett; quilted by Karen Williamson

FINISHED QUILT: 62½" x 69½"  ■  FINISHED BLOCK: 7" x 7"

*Continued from page 47*

### From the light-green solid, cut:
13 strips, 2⅛" x 42"; crosscut into 224 squares, 2⅛" x 2⅛"

### From the red-and-white print, cut:
6 strips, 1½" x 42"
7 strips, 2½" x 42"

### From the blue floral, cut:
7 strips, 6" x 42"

## BLOCK ASSEMBLY

For each block, you'll need two print 2¼" x 4" rectangles and two print 2¼" x 5¾" rectangles, all matching.

1. Sew print 2¼" x 4" rectangles to each side of a white 2¼" x 4" rectangle as shown. Press the seam allowances toward the print rectangles. Make one for each block.

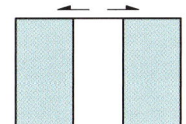

Make 1.

2. Sew print 2¼" x 5¾" rectangles to the top and bottom edges of the unit from step 1. Press the seam allowances toward the just-added rectangles. Make one for each block.

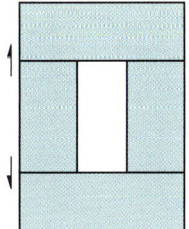

Make 1.

3. Referring to "Folded-Corner Units" on page 7, sew a white square to each corner of the unit from step 2. Press the seam allowances toward the white triangles. Make one for each block.

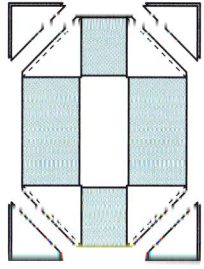 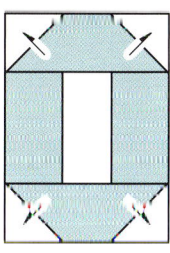

Make 1.

4. Sew a white 1⅜" x 7½" rectangle to each side of the unit from step 3. Press the seam allowances toward the white rectangles. Make one for each block.

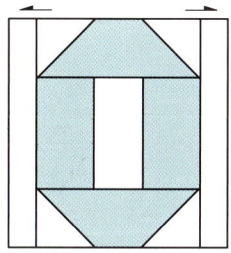

Make 1.

5. Using the folded-corner technique, sew a light-green square to each corner of the unit from step 4. Press the seam allowances toward the light-green triangles. Make a total of 56 blocks.

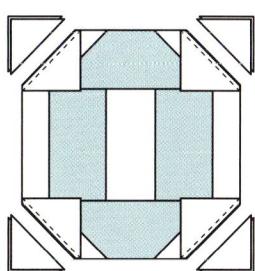 

Make 56.

*Candy Bracelet*

## QUILT ASSEMBLY AND FINISHING

For help with any of the finishing steps, go to ShopMartingale.com/HowtoQuilt for free, downloadable instructions.

1. Arrange the blocks in eight horizontal rows of seven blocks each, rotating every other block a quarter turn. Sew the blocks together in rows, pressing the seam allowances as shown. Join the rows. Press the seam allowances in one direction.

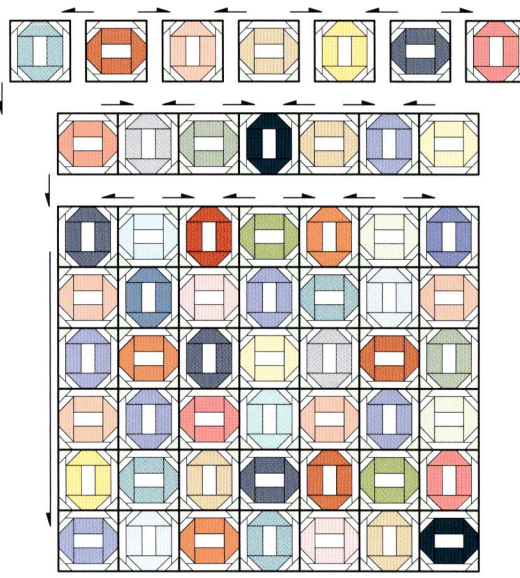

Quilt assembly

2. Referring to "Butted-Corner Borders" on page 76, add the red-and-white 1½"-wide strips for the inner border and the floral 6"-wide strips for the outer border.

3. Layer the quilt top, batting, and backing; baste the layers together. Quilt as desired.

4. Using the red-and-white 2½"-wide strips, bind the edges of the quilt.

5. Add a label.

# Off Course

*Strip piecing makes this quilt super easy to make. Although the blocks look like they contain a lot of pieces, once you sew the strips together and crosscut them into segments, you only have to join 12 rectangles for each block.*

## MATERIALS

*Yardage is based on 42"-wide fabric.*

30 strips, 2½" x 42", of assorted dark prints for blocks
2 yards of white solid for blocks and border
⅝ yard of multicolored floral for binding
4 yards of fabric for backing
59" x 71" piece of batting

## CUTTING FROM PRECUTS AND YARDAGE

**From the white solid, cut:**
30 strips, 1½" x 42"
6 strips, 3½" x 42"

**From the multicolored floral, cut**
7 strips, 2½" x 42"

## STRIP PIECING

1. Sew a dark 2½"-wide strip to the long side of a white 1½"-wide strip. Press the seam allowances in either direction. (I pressed the seam allowances toward the white strips, but if you're concerned about "shadowing," press the seam allowances toward the dark strips.) Make 30 strip sets.

Make 30.

## CUTTING FROM SCRAPS

*If you prefer to use scraps instead of precuts, follow the instructions below. See "Cutting from Precuts and Yardage" at left for instructions on cutting the borders and binding.*

**From assorted dark prints, cut:**
80 rectangles, 2½" x 6½"
160 rectangles, 2½" x 3½"

**From assorted light prints, cut:**
80 rectangles, 1½" x 6½"
160 rectangles, 2½" x 3½"

Instead of making strip sets as directed in the instructions, sew the light and dark rectangles together as shown to make the number of units indicated for each block.

 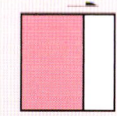

Make 4 for each block.  Make 8 for each block.

Then follow the directions in "Block Assembly" on page 53 for constructing the blocks.

"Off Course," pieced and quilted by Kim Brackett

**FINISHED QUILT: 54½" x 66½"** ▪ **FINISHED BLOCK: 12" x 12"**

2. Crosscut *each* of 23 strip sets into three 3½" x 6½" segments (69 total) and five 3½" x 3½" segments (115 total).

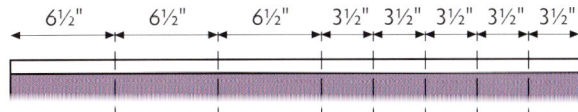

3. Crosscut *each* of the remaining seven strip sets into two 3½" x 6½" segments (14 total) and seven 3½" x 3½" segments (49 total). You'll have three 3½" x 6½" and four 3½" x 3½" segments left over.

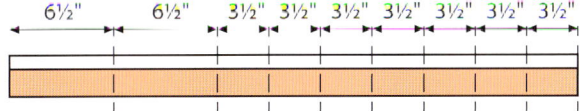

## BLOCK ASSEMBLY

1. Sew two different 3½" x 3½" segments together as shown. Press the seam allowances in the direction indicated. Make four for each block.

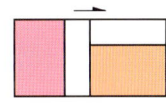

Make 4.

2. Sew a 3½" x 6½" segment to the top of the unit from step 1. Press the seam allowances toward the just-added unit. Make four for each block.

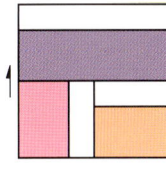

Make 4.

3. Sew four units from step 2 together as shown above right. Referring to "Pressing" on page 76, press the seam allowances in a clockwise direction. Make a total of 20 blocks.

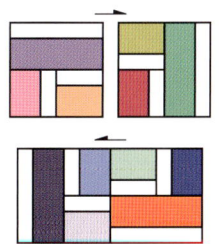
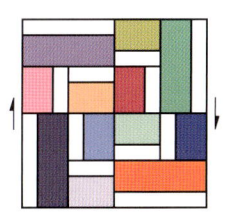

Make 20.

## QUILT ASSEMBLY AND FINISHING

For help with any of the finishing steps, go to ShopMartingale.com/HowtoQuilt for free, downloadable instructions.

1. Arrange the blocks in five horizontal rows of four blocks each. Sew the blocks together in rows, pressing the seam allowances in alternating directions. Sew the rows together. Press the seam allowances in one direction.

Quilt assembly

2. Referring to "Butted-Corner Borders" on page 76, add the white 3½"-wide strips for the border.

3. Layer the quilt top, batting, and backing; baste the layers together. Quilt as desired.

4. Using the multicolored floral 2½"-wide strips, bind the edges of the quilt.

5. Add a label.

*Off Course* 53

# Gypsy

*I really enjoy piecing when there are no opposing seam allowances slowing me down. The offset rows in this quilt allow you to sew without matching every seam. Try to maintain the vertical alignment that travels along the length of the quilt, but if you're off by just a tad, no one will notice!*

## MATERIALS

*Yardage is based on 42"-wide fabric.*

23 strips, 2½" x 42", of assorted medium to dark print for blocks
1⅝ yards of taupe solid for blocks
1⅛ yards of large-scale floral for outer border
⅞ yard of pink print for inner border and binding
4 yards of fabric for backing
66" x 73" piece of batting

## CUTTING FROM PRECUTS AND YARDAGE

**From *each* of 18 assorted medium- to dark-print strips, cut:**
1 square, 2½" x 2½" (18 total)
2 strips, 2½" x 18" (36 total)

**From *each* of the remaining 5 assorted medium- to dark-print strips, cut:**
2 strips, 2½" x 18" (10 total)

*Continued on page 56*

## CUTTING FROM SCRAPS

*If you prefer to use scraps instead of precuts, follow the instructions below. See "Cutting from Precuts and Yardage" at left for instructions on cutting the borders and binding.*

**From assorted medium to dark prints, cut:**
324 squares, 2½" x 2½"

**From background fabric, cut:**
80 rectangles, 2½" x 4½"
134 squares, 2½" x 2½"

Sew the squares and rectangles together as shown in steps 3 through 6 for constructing rows A, B, C, and D on pages 56 and 57.

*"Gypsy," pieced and quilted by Kim Brackett*
**FINISHED QUILT: 61½" x 63½"**

*Continued from page 54*

### From the taupe solid, cut:
1 strip, 2½" x 42"; crosscut into 12 squares,
 2½" x 2½"
9 strips, 2½" x 42"; crosscut *each* strip into:
 1 square, 2½" x 2½" (9 total)
 2 strips, 2½" x 18" (18 total, 1 is extra)
6 strips, 4½" x 42"; crosscut the strips in half to
 yield 12 strips, 4½" x 18"

### From the pink print, cut:
6 strips, 1½" x 42"
7 strips, 2½" x 42"

### From the large-scale floral, cut:
6 strips, 6" x 42"

## ROW ASSEMBLY

1. Select 12 different print strips. Sew each print strip to a taupe 4½"-wide strip. Press the seam allowances in either direction. Make 12 strip sets. Crosscut *each* strip set into seven 2½"-wide segments (84 total). You'll have four segments left over.

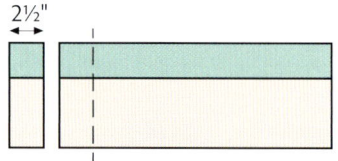

Make 12 strip sets.
Cut 7 segments from each strip set.

2. Sew two print and one taupe 2½"-wide strip together as shown. Press the seam allowances in either direction. Make 17 strip sets. Crosscut *each* strip set into seven 2½"-wide segments (119 total). You'll have six segments left over.

Make 17 strip sets.
Cut 7 segments from each strip set.

3. To make row A, join one taupe square and eight segments from step 1 as shown. Press the seam allowances in either direction. Make six rows.

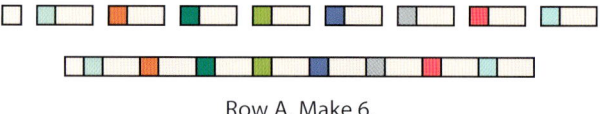

Row A. Make 6.

4. To make row B, join one taupe square and eight segments from step 2 as shown. Press the seam allowances in either direction. Make eight rows.

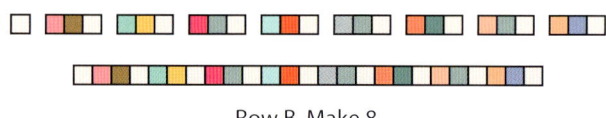

Row B. Make 8.

5. To make row C, join two print squares, one taupe square, and seven segments from step 2 as shown. Press the seam allowances in either direction. Make seven rows.

Row C. Make 7.

*Scrap-Basket Strips and Squares*

6. To make row D, join one print square and eight units from step 1 as shown. Press the seam allowances in either direction. Make four rows.

Row D. Make 4.

## QUILT ASSEMBLY AND FINISHING

For help with any of the finishing steps, go to ShopMartingale.com/HowtoQuilt for free, downloadable instructions.

1. Arrange the A, B, C, and D rows as shown below. Fold a few of the print squares in the top row in half and finger-press. Align each crease with a seam between two print squares in the second row to maintain the pattern. Sew the rows together, pressing the seam allowances in one direction. The uneven edges of the quilt top will be trimmed in the next step.

Quilt assembly

2. Use a rotary cutter and an acrylic ruler to trim the sides of the quilt top even with the outer edges of the C rows.

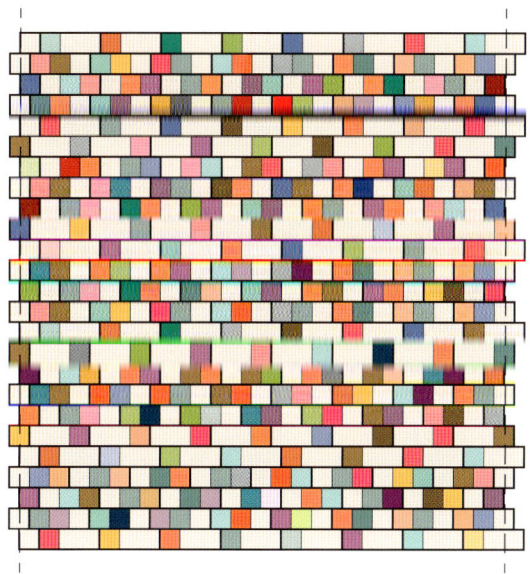

Trim quilt top edges even with C rows.

3. Referring to "Butted-Corner Borders" on page 76, add the pink 1½"-wide strips for the inner border and the floral strips for the outer border.

4. Layer the quilt top, batting, and backing; baste the layers together. Quilt as desired.

5. Using the pink 2½"-wide strips, bind the edges of the quilt.

6. Add a label.

*Gypsy* 57

# Touch a Star

*The stars in this design appear to overlap, creating an interesting and complex-looking pattern. If you look closely, you may be able to tell that the blocks aren't actually stars, but a combination of simple blocks that, when joined together, form the stars. We'll just let that be our secret.*

## MATERIALS

*Yardage is based on 42"-wide fabric.*

24 strips, 2½" x 42", of assorted prints for blocks
2⅝ yards of cream solid for blocks
1⅛ yards of large-scale floral for outer border
⅞ yard of green print for inner border and binding
4¼ yards of fabric for backing
66" x 74" piece of batting

## CUTTING FROM PRECUTS AND YARDAGE

**From *each* of the assorted print strips, cut:**
6 rectangles, 2½" x 6½" (144 total; 2 are extra)

**From the cream solid, cut:**
6 strips, 4½" x 42"; crosscut into 42 squares, 4½" x 4½"
23 strips, 2½" x 42"; crosscut into:
    26 rectangles, 2½" x 6½"
    284 squares, 2½" x 2½"

**From the green print, cut:**
6 strips, 1½" x 42"
7 strips, 2½" x 42"

**From the large-scale floral, cut:**
6 strips, 6" x 42"

## CUTTING FROM SCRAPS

*If you prefer to use scraps instead of precuts, follow the instructions below. See "Cutting from Precuts and Yardage" at left for instructions on cutting the borders and binding.*

**From assorted dark prints, cut:**
142 rectangles, 2½" x 6½"

**From assorted light prints, cut:**
42 squares, 4½" x 4½"
26 rectangles, 2½" x 6½"
284 squares, 2½" x 2½"

*"Touch a Star,"* pieced and quilted by Karen Williamson

**FINISHED QUILT: 61½" x 69½"** ▪ **FINISHED BLOCK: 8" x 8"**

## BLOCK ASSEMBLY

1. Referring to "Folded-Corner Units" on page 7, make a folded-corner unit as shown, using two cream 2½" squares and a print rectangle. Press the seam allowances toward the cream triangles. Make 142 folded-corner units.

   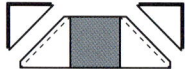 
   Make 142.

2. Using a partial seam, sew a cream 4½" square to a unit from step 1, starting at the outer edge and stopping about halfway across the square with a backstitch. Press the seam allowances away from the center square.

   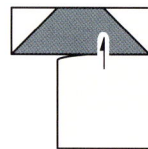

3. Sew three more units to the center square in the order shown. Press the seam allowances away from the center square. After the last unit is attached, complete the partial seam to make a center block. Press all seam allowances away from the square. Make a total of 20 blocks.

   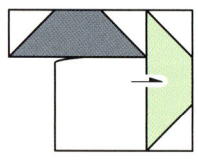 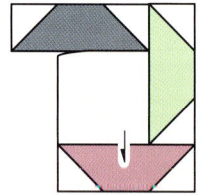

   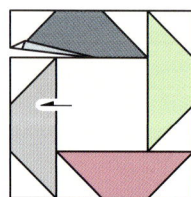 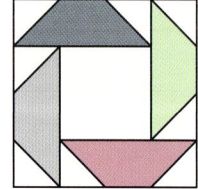

   Center block.
   Make 20.

4. Repeat steps 2 and 3, starting with a cream rectangle and adding three units from step 1 to a cream 4½" square as shown. Press all seam allowances away from the center square. Make 18 edge blocks.

   Edge block.
   Make 18.

5. Repeat steps 2 and 3, using two cream rectangles, two units from step 1, and one cream 4½" square as shown. Press all seam allowances away from the center square. Make four corner blocks.

   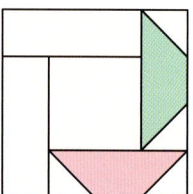

   Corner block.
   Make 4.

## QUILT ASSEMBLY AND FINISHING

For help with any of the finishing steps, go to ShopMartingale.com/HowtoQuilt for free, downloadable instructions.

1. Arrange the center blocks, edge blocks, and corner blocks in seven horizontal rows of six blocks each as shown. Sew the blocks together in rows, pressing the seam allowances in alternating directions from row to row. Join the rows. Press the seam allowances in one direction.

Quilt assembly

2. Referring to "Butted-Corner Borders" on page 76, add the green 1½"-wide strips for the inner border and the floral strips for the outer border.
3. Layer the quilt top, batting, and backing; baste the layers together. Quilt as desired.
4. Using the green 2½"-wide strips, bind the edges of the quilt.
5. Add a label.

# Simplicity

"Basic" fabrics are typically those that have a subtle pattern and are used to blend with other prints. I used many colors of different basic prints in this quilt, and I really like the way the colorful but subtle fabrics strengthen the design.

## MATERIALS

*Yardage is based on 42"-wide fabric.*

24 strips, 2½" x 42", of assorted dark prints for blocks
2½ yards of cream solid for blocks and binding
3½ yards of fabric for backing
53" x 65" piece of batting

## CUTTING FROM PRECUTS AND YARDAGE

**From *each* of 16 assorted dark-print strips, cut:**
5 rectangles, 2½" x 4½" (80 total)
6 squares, 2½" x 2½" (96 total)

**From *each* of 8 assorted dark-print strips, cut:**
6 rectangles, 2½" x 4½" (48 total)
4 squares, 2½" x 2½" (32 total)

**From the cream solid, cut:**
7 strips, 6½" x 42"; crosscut into:
    32 rectangles, 4½" x 6½"
    48 rectangles, 2½" x 6½"
14 strips, 2½" x 42"; crosscut 8 *of the strips* into 128 squares, 2½" x 2½". (Set aside the remaining 6 strips for binding.)

## CUTTING FROM SCRAPS

*If you prefer to use scraps instead of precuts, follow the instructions below. See "Cutting from Precuts and Yardage" at left for instructions on cutting the borders and binding.*

**From assorted dark prints, cut:**
128 rectangles, 2½" x 4½"
128 squares, 2½" x 2½"

**From assorted light prints, cut:**
32 rectangles, 4½" x 6½"
48 rectangles, 2½" x 6½"
128 squares, 2½" x 2½"

*"Simplicity,"* pieced and quilted by Kim Brackett

**FINISHED QUILT: 48½" x 60½" • FINISHED BLOCK: 6" x 6"**

## BLOCK ASSEMBLY

1. Join a dark rectangle to a cream square. Press the seam allowances toward the dark rectangle. Make 128 units.

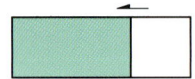

Make 128.

2. Referring to "Folded-Corner Units" on page 7, make a folded-corner unit as shown, using a cream 4½" x 6½" rectangle and a dark square. Press the seam allowances toward the dark triangle. Make 32 folded-corner units.

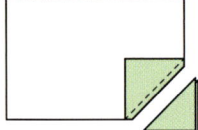 

Make 32.

3. Make a folded-corner unit using a cream 2½" x 6½" rectangle and two different dark squares. Press the seam allowances toward the dark triangles. Make 48 folded-corner units.

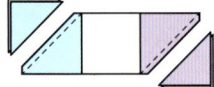 

Make 48.

4. Join a unit from step 1 and a unit from step 2 to make an edge block. Press the seam allowances as indicated. Make a total of 32 edge blocks.

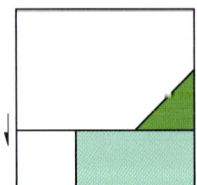

Edge block.
Make 32.

5. Join two units from step 1 and a unit from step 3 as shown to make a center block. Press the seam allowances as indicated. Make a total of 48 center blocks.

Center block. Make 48.

## QUILT ASSEMBLY AND FINISHING

For help with any of the finishing steps, go to ShopMartingale.com/HowtoQuilt for free, downloadable instructions.

1. Arrange the center and edge blocks in 10 horizontal rows of eight blocks each as shown, placing the edge blocks around the outside edges. Sew the blocks together in rows. Join the rows. Press the seam allowances as indicated.

Quilt assembly

2. Layer the quilt top, batting, and backing; baste the layers together. Quilt as desired.
3. Using the cream 2½"-wide strips, bind the edges of the quilt.
4. Add a label.

*Scrap-Basket Strips and Squares*

# Aviary

*Although I chose lighter fabrics for the main design and a darker fabric for the background, I can imagine this quilt would be gorgeous in many different fabric and color combinations. And rotating the blocks in different layouts will give you even more design options.*

## MATERIALS

*Yardage is based on 42"-wide fabric.*

24 strips, 2½" x 42", of assorted light to medium prints in pink, orange, aqua, and green for blocks
1⅞ yards of green solid for blocks
1⅓ yards of large-scale floral for outer border
1 yard of aqua print for inner border and binding
5 yards of fabric for backing
66" x 82" piece of batting

## CUTTING FROM PRECUTS AND YARDAGE

**From each of the assorted light to medium print strips, cut:**
6 rectangles, 2½" x 4½" (144 total)
4 squares, 2½" x 2½" (96 total)

**From the green solid, cut:**
24 strips, 2½" x 42"; crosscut into:
    144 rectangles, 2½" x 4½"
    96 squares, 2½" x 2½"

**From the aqua print, cut:**
6 strips, 1½" x 42"
8 strips, 2½" x 42"

**From the large-scale floral, cut:**
7 strips, 6" x 42"

## CUTTING FROM SCRAPS

*If you prefer to use scraps instead of precuts, follow the instructions below. See "Cutting from Precuts and Yardage" at left for instructions on cutting the borders and binding.*

**From assorted light (main) prints, cut:**
144 rectangles, 2½" x 4½"
96 squares, 2½" x 2½"

**From assorted dark (background) prints, cut:**
144 rectangles, 2½" x 4½"
96 squares, 2½" x 2½"

"Aviary," pieced and quilted by Kim Brackett

FINISHED QUILT: 61½" x 77½" ▪ FINISHED BLOCK: 8" x 8"

## BLOCK ASSEMBLY

1. Sew a green rectangle to a print rectangle. Press the seam allowances toward the green rectangle. Make 96.

   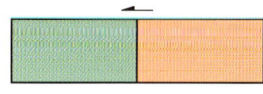
   Make 96.

2. Sew green squares to each end of a print rectangle as shown. Press the seam allowances toward the green squares. Make 48.

   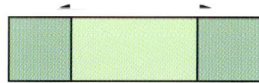
   Make 48.

3. Sew two different print squares to each end of a green rectangle. Press the seam allowances as indicated. Make 48.

   Make 48.

4. Lay out two units from step 1, one unit from step 2, and one unit from step 3 as shown. Join the units and press the seam allowances as shown. Make 48 blocks.

   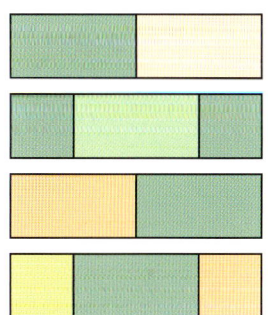 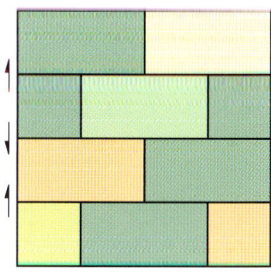
   Make 48.

## QUILT ASSEMBLY AND FINISHING

For help with any of the finishing steps, go to ShopMartingale.com/HowtoQuilt for free, downloadable instructions.

1. Arrange the blocks in eight horizontal rows of six blocks each as shown. Sew the blocks together in rows, pressing the seam allowances as shown. Sew the rows together. Press the seam allowances in one direction.

   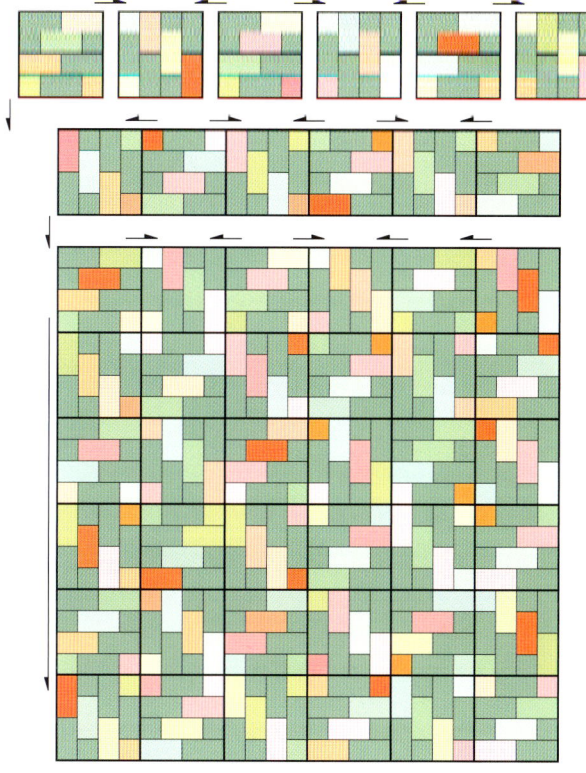
   Quilt assembly

2. Referring to "Butted-Corner Borders" on page 76, add the aqua 1½"-wide strips for the inner border and the floral strips for the outer border.

3. Layer the quilt top, batting, and backing; baste the layers together. Quilt as desired.

4. Using the aqua 2½"-wide strips, bind the edges of the quilt.

5. Add a label.

*Aviary*

# Wildflowers

*Candy-colored prints sparkle in this field of hexagon wildflowers. While 12 wedges come together in the center of each block, you don't worry about perfection. My secret? Trim away the center and appliqué a contrasting circle over the top for stress-free sewing and fun results.*

## MATERIALS

*Yardage is based on 42"-wide fabric.*

49 strips, 2½" x 42", of assorted dark prints for blocks
49 strips, 2½" x 42", of assorted light prints for blocks
½ yard of red print for binding
3⅝ yards of fabric for backing
55" x 67" piece of batting
2" x 4" piece of template plastic
Fine-tip permanent marker
Pencil for marking fabric
Appliqué needle
Neutral-colored thread for appliqué

## CUTTING FROM PRECUTS AND YARDAGE

*The cutting measurements provided ensure that you'll be able to cut the required number of pieces from each 2½" strip; however, if you cut carefully, you should be able to cut an extra set of rectangles from each strip. See the piece count in the "Cutting from Scraps" box at right.*

**From *each* of 37 assorted light-print strips, cut:**
6 rectangles, 2½" x 4⅜" (222 total)

**From *each* of 12 assorted light-print strips, cut:**
8 rectangles, 2½" x 4⅜" (96 total)

*Continued on page 70*

## CUTTING FROM SCRAPS

*If you prefer to use scraps instead of precuts, follow the instructions below. See "Cutting from Precuts and Yardage" at left for instructions on cutting the borders and binding.*

**From assorted light prints, cut:**
98 matching sets of 3 rectangles, 2½" x 4⅜"
12 matching sets of 2 rectangles, 2½" x 4⅜"

**From assorted dark prints, cut:**
98 matching sets of 3 rectangles, 2½" x 4⅜"
12 matching sets of 2 rectangles, 2½" x 4⅜"
110 squares, 2½" x 2½"

*"Wildflowers," pieced and quilted by Kim Brackett*

**FINISHED QUILT: 50½" x 62¼"  ▪  FINISHED BLOCK: 6¼" x 7⅛"**

*Continued from page 68*

**From *each* of 25 assorted dark-print strips, cut:**
6 rectangles, 2½" x 4⅜" (150 total)
2 squares, 2½" x 2½" (50 total)

**From *each* of 12 assorted dark-print strips, cut:**
8 rectangles, 2½" x 4⅜" (96 total)
2 squares, 2½" x 2½" (24 total)

**From *each* of 12 assorted dark-print strips, cut:**
6 rectangles, 2½" x 4⅜" (72 total)
3 squares, 2½" x 2½" (36 total)

**From the red print, cut:**
6 strips, 2½" x 42"

## SPECIAL CUTTING

1. Carefully stack three or four light rectangles, right sides up. Cut the rectangles in half diagonally from the bottom-left corner to the upper-right corner as shown. Without disturbing the stacked fabrics, place a ruler on each stack and align the 3" line with the end of each stack. Place the 2½" line on the ruler on the bottom of the stack as shown. Trim off the points of the triangles creating a trapezoid shape. Cut the remaining light rectangles in the same manner.

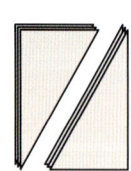 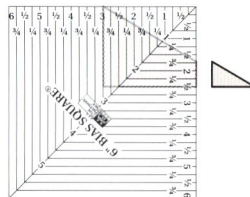

2. Stack three or four dark rectangles, right sides up. Cut the rectangles in half diagonally from the bottom-right corner to the upper-left corner as shown. Without disturbing the stacked fabrics, place a ruler on each stack and align the 3" line with the end of each stack. Align the edge of the ruler with the top of the stack as shown. Trim off the points of the triangles creating a trapezoid shape that mirrors the trapezoid from step 1. Then cut the remaining dark rectangles in the same manner.

 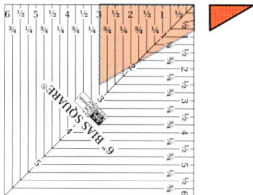

## BLOCK ASSEMBLY

1. Sew a light and a dark trapezoid together as shown. Press the seam allowances open to reduce bulk. Make six identical units.

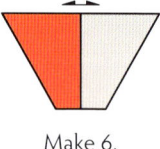

Make 6.

*Scrap-Basket Strips and Squares*

2. Join three units from step 1, pressing the seam allowances open. Make two half blocks. There's no need to trim the points that extend from the seam allowances—the points will make it easier to align the blocks when assembling the quilt.

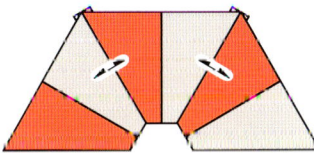

Make 6.

3. Sew the half blocks from step 2 together to make a center block. Press the seam allowances open. Make a total of 98 blocks.

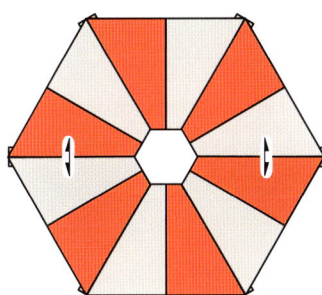

Make 98.

4. To make the edge blocks, repeat step 1 to make three identical units. Join the units as described in step 2 to make an edge block. Make a total of 12 blocks. (You'll have 12 dark and 12 light trapezoids left over.)

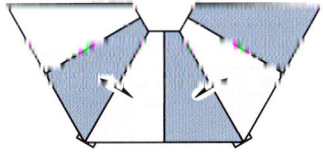

Make 12.

## APPLIQUÉ

1. Trace patterns A and B on page 74 onto the template plastic using a fine-tip permanent marker. Cut out the templates exactly on the drawn line.

2. Place template A on the right side of a dark square. Use a pencil to lightly trace around the template. Cut out the circle ¼" outside the drawn line. Cut out 98 circles.

3. Place template B on the right side of a dark square. Repeating step 2, trace and cut out 12 half circles.

4. Place a dark circle in the center of a center block and pin in place.

5. Cut a single strand of thread approximately 18" long. Thread an appliqué needle and tie a knot in one end. Use the tip of the needle to turn under the seam allowance along the marked line. Hold the turned seam allowance firmly with your thumb and first finger of your free hand. Hide your knot in the fold made by the seam allowance, bringing the needle out along the folded edge. Insert the needle into the pieced block, directly below where the needle emerged. Run the needle not more than ⅛" under the block. Bring the needle up through the block, catching one or two threads of the circle's folded edge. Continue in the same way until the entire circle is stitched in place. To secure the stitching, insert the needle through the pieced block and make several small stitches in the back of the pieced block. Make a total of 98 blocks.

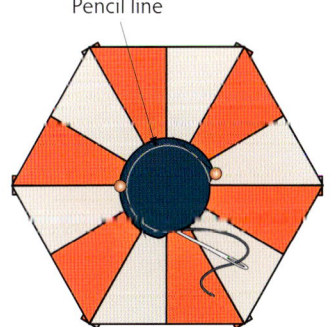

Pencil line

*Wildflowers*

6. Place a half circle on an edge block, aligning the straight edge of the half circle with the long side of the block. Repeat step 5 to appliqué the half circle in place. The straight edge of the half circle will not be appliquéd since it will be along the outer edge of the quilt top. Make 12 blocks.

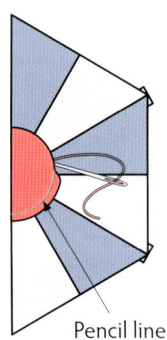
Pencil line

## ROW ASSEMBLY

1. Starting one or two threads from the seam line with a backstitch, sew two blocks together as shown. Stop stitching one or two threads from the seam line with a backstitch.

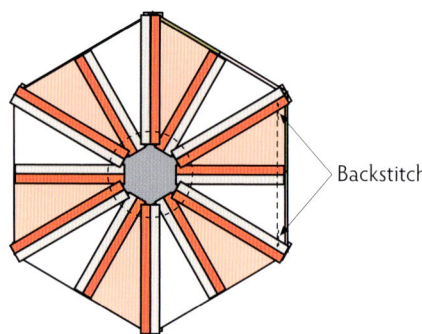
Backstitch

2. Sew eight center blocks together as shown to make row. Press the seam allowances as indicated. Make a total of seven rows.

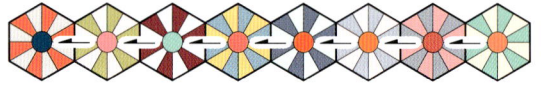
Make 7.

3. Join seven center blocks and two edge blocks as shown to make a row. Press the seam allowances as indicated. Make a total of six rows.

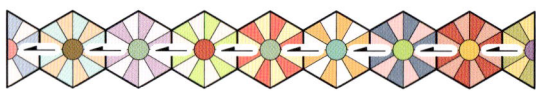
Make 6.

## QUILT ASSEMBLY AND FINISHING

For help with any of the finishing steps, go to ShopMartingale.com/HowtoQuilt for free, downloadable instructions.

1. Lay out two rows as shown. Sew the bottom of the first row to the top of the second row, stitching the sides of the blocks together as described in step 1 of "Row Assembly." Continue joining the blocks, sewing one seam at a time, to make a two-row section. Do not press the seam allowances until the section is complete. Then press the seam allowances in alternating directions from block to block.

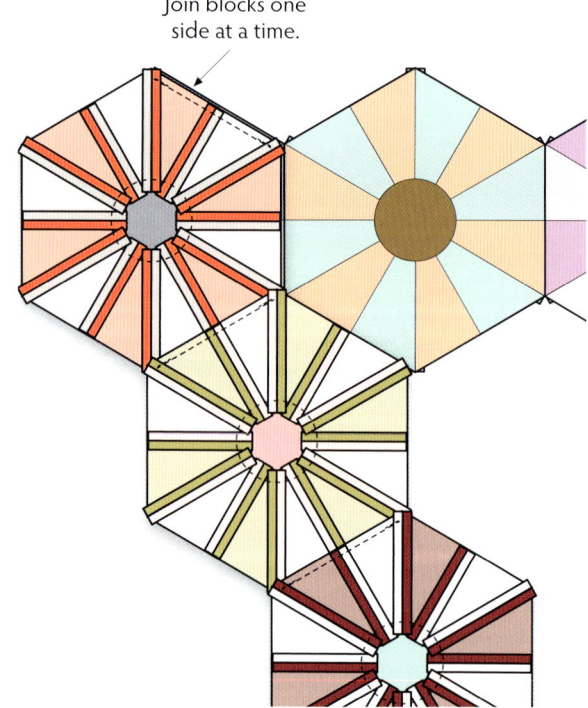
Join blocks one side at a time.

2. Continue adding rows, alternating them as shown in the photo on page 69, until all the rows are joined. Press the seam allowances in alternating directions.

3. Place the long edge of an acrylic ruler along the top row of the quilt top where the blocks form a V as shown. Trim the top row to make a straight edge. In the same way, trim the bottom row.

4. Layer the quilt top, batting, and backing; baste the layers together. Quilt as desired.

5. Using the red 2½"-wide strips, bind the edges of the quilt.

6. Add a label.

Wildflowers 73

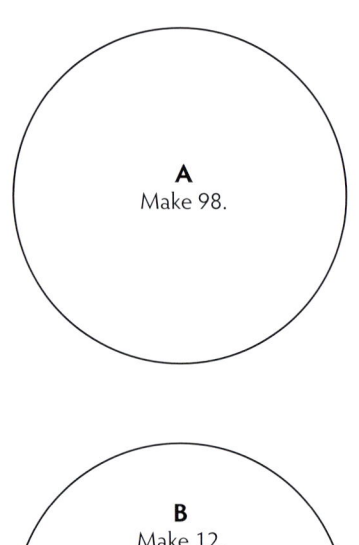

**A**
Make 98.

**B**
Make 12.

Patterns do not include seam allowances. Add ¼" seam allowance for needle-turn appliqué.

# TOOLS AND SUPPLIES

**Listed in this section are basic materials and supplies used to make the quilts in this book.** I've indicated some of my personal preferences, but you may want to experiment with other rulers, threads, and tools to determine your own favorites.

**Acrylic rotary-cutting rulers:** I recommend a 6" x 24" ruler for cutting across the width of the fabric. A large square ruler (10" or larger) is helpful when cutting 10" squares from your scraps or stash fabrics. A 6½" square ruler with a 45° line is perfect for crosscutting the strips into smaller segments, trimming half-square-triangle units and for marking the sewing lines on folded-corner units (see "Folded-Corner Units" on page 7).

**Fine-lead mechanical pencil:** I prefer this kind of pencil for marking sewing lines on folded-corner units.

**Iron and ironing board:** A steam iron is helpful when ironing fabric before cutting and pressing seam allowances.

**Measuring tape:** I "borrowed" my husband's metal measuring tape a few years ago. It's very useful for measuring fabric lengths and batting and for measuring quilts when adding borders.

**Painter's tape:** Use painter's tape for making a temporary sewing guide on your machine for folded-corner units. I also use it to tape down the backing when layering and basting in preparation for quilting.

**Pins:** Use glass-head pins or quilter's pins with a thin shank.

**Rotary cutter and mat:** If the blade on your rotary cutter doesn't close automatically, develop the habit of closing it when it's not in use (for your own safety). A sharp blade will make cutting much easier. Use your rotary cutter on a self-healing mat designed for cutting. Keep the cutter and mat clean and free of dust to prolong the life of your blade and mat.

**Seam ripper:** Any type of seam ripper will work as long as it's sharp enough to cut the thread without distorting the fabric. Hopefully you won't need to use it!

**Sewing machine:** Have your machine serviced regularly; clean it often according to the manufacturer's instructions.

**Sewing machine needles:** I like to use a size 80/12 Sharp or Universal needle for piecing.

**Sharp scissors:** Use sewing shears for cutting fabric. Keep a small pair of scissors close to your sewing machine for clipping threads.

**Spray starch:** I use spray starch when ironing fabric to remove wrinkles and for adding body and stability to the fabric before cutting strips and squares.

**Thread:** Use a high-quality cotton thread for piecing. I like to use tan or gray for piecing scrap quilts. These neutral colors blend well with multiple fabrics.

**Walking foot:** In addition to being useful for machine quilting, a walking foot is also good for attaching binding to your finished quilt. If your sewing machine didn't come equipped with this attachment, your local sewing machine dealer can help you find one that will fit your machine.

# BASIC QUILTMAKING INSTRUCTIONS

**This section outlines basic skills and techniques necessary for making quilts.**
Often in quiltmaking, there are many different ways to accomplish the same task. These are the methods I prefer, but I suggest you experiment with other methods to determine which work best for you and provide more enjoyment as you make your quilt.

## PRESSING

To press seam allowances after sewing, lay the unopened unit on your ironing board. Press the sewn seam flat by moving your iron in an up-and-down motion. Open the unit and press the seam allowances in the desired direction.

The project instructions indicate the direction to press seam allowances. Illustrations are provided as well, with the pressing direction indicated by arrows. If it doesn't matter which way the seam allowances are pressed, the instructions will direct you to "press the seam allowances in either direction."

To reduce bulk where multiple seam allowances meet, I like to press the seam allowances in a clockwise or counterclockwise direction. Using a seam ripper, remove the stitching above the horizontal seam allowance as shown.

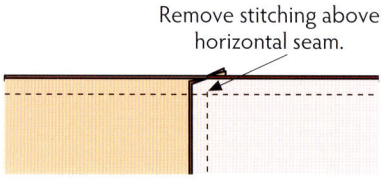
Remove stitching above horizontal seam.

From the back of the block, use your thumb and forefinger to finger-press the seam allowances in the direction indicated. Turn the block over and press from the front with an iron.

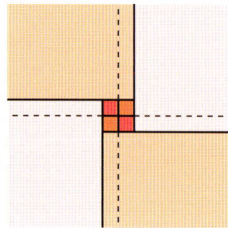

## ADDING BORDERS

Adding borders to your quilts serves multiple purposes. Plain borders can stop the chaos in the center of a busy quilt by providing a visual resting place. They also add extra width and length to your quilt without the necessity of piecing extra blocks. Pieced borders can add an interesting design element to the outside edges of your quilt. Whatever your intent may be for adding borders, take time to measure to ensure a successful outcome.

### Butted-Corner Borders

1. Smooth out your pieced quilt top as flat as possible. Measure the length of the quilt top through the center. Use this measurement to cut border strips for both sides of the quilt top, piecing the strips as necessary. Mark the center along the side edges of the quilt top and mark the center of the border strips along one long edge using a pencil. Pin the border strips, right sides together, to the side edges

of the quilt top at the center marks and the ends. Finish pinning the border strips in place. Sew the side-border strips to the quilt top and press the seam allowances toward the borders unless otherwise indicated.

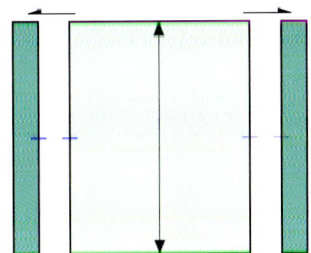

Measure center of quilt,
top to bottom. Mark centers.

2. Measure the width of the quilt top, including the side borders. Use this measurement to cut borders for the top and bottom edges of the quilt top. Piece the border strips if necessary. Mark the center of the top and bottom edges of the quilt top and mark the center of the border strips along one long side using a pencil. Pin the border strips, right sides together, to the top and bottom edges of the quilt top at the center marks and the ends. Finish pinning the border strips in place. Sew the top- and bottom-border strips to the quilt top, and press the seam allowances toward the borders unless otherwise indicated.

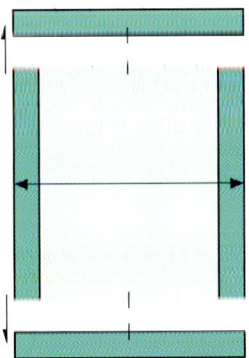

Measure center of quilt, side to side,
including border strips. Mark centers.

3. Repeat steps 1 and 2 if your quilt has multiple butted-corner borders.

## Mitered-Corner Borders

Mitered corners can add amazing visual effects when using directional fabrics, special border prints, and striped fabrics. The design meets precisely at the corners and seems to encircle the quilt. When adding multiple borders, sew the border strips together first, and then cut the border in one piece as you would for a single border.

1. Measure the length of the quilt top. Multiply the width of the cut border strip by 2 and add that number to the measurement of your quilt top. Add about 4" to this measurement just to be sure your strips will be long enough for the mitered corner. (It's much easier to trim than to add!)

2. Measure the width of the quilt top. Multiply the width of the cut border strip by 2 and add that number to the measurement of your quilt top. Add about 4" to this measurement just to be sure your strips will be long enough for the mitered corner.

3. Measure to find the center of each edge of the quilt top and lightly mark with a pencil.

4. Fold a border strip in half and pencil-mark the edge at the center. Measure out on each side of the center mark, half the length of the quilt top, and pencil-mark the edge of the border to mark the length of the quilt top. Pin the border strip to the side edge, matching the top and bottom edges of the quilt top with the pencil marks near the ends of the border strip and matching the center pencil mark on the quilt top with the center mark on the border strip.

*Basic Quiltmaking Instructions* 77

5. Begin sewing ¼" from the edge of the quilt top. Stop sewing ¼" from the opposite end of the quilt top, backstitching to secure the seams at the beginning and end.

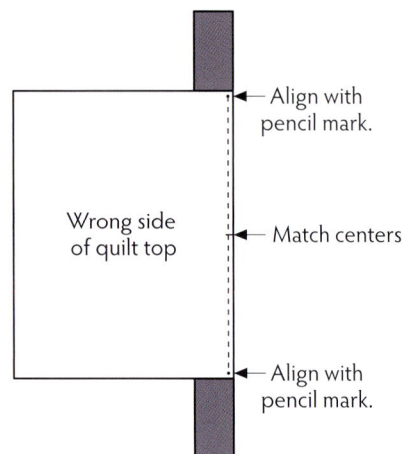

6. Repeat steps 4 and 5 to add the remaining side border, and then add the top and bottom borders in the same manner. Press the seam allowances toward the borders.

7. After the borders have been sewn to the quilt top, fold the quilt top diagonally with the right sides together as shown. Align the seams and the edges of the borders as evenly as possible. Finger-press the seam allowances of the border away from you. Place pins in the border and on the fold as shown.

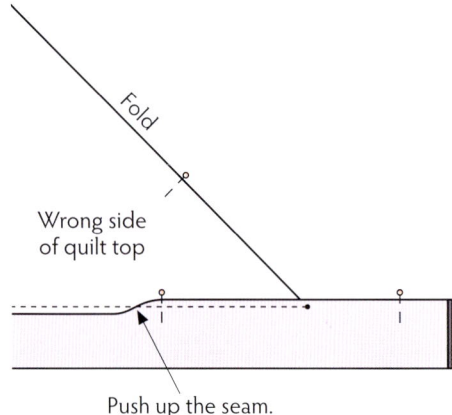

8. Align a ruler along the edge of the fold, with the 45° line along the edge of the border. With a pencil, draw a line across the border along the ruler. Place pins on the drawn line to keep the fabric from shifting.

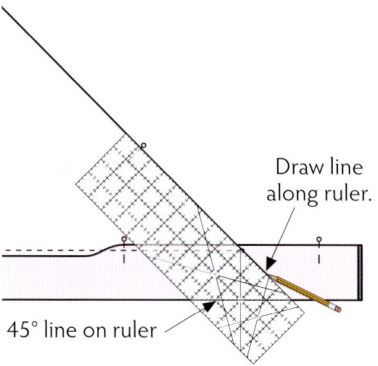

9. Begin sewing on the drawn line, backstitching at the beginning to secure the stitching. Continue to sew until you reach the edge of the border, and then backstitch to secure.

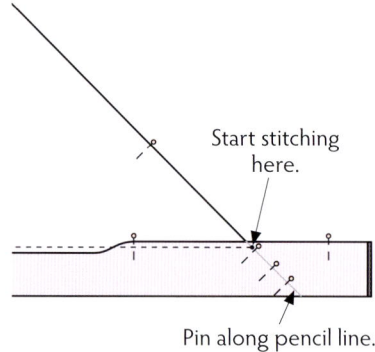

10. Unfold the quilt to check the accuracy of your miter. Trim the excess fabric away, leaving a ¼" seam allowance. Press the seam allowances in either direction and press the border seam allowances back in place. Repeat from step 7 to miter the remaining corners.

# RESOURCES

Refer to the listings below to find out where you can purchase fabric and batting for making the quilts in this book.

## FABRICS

**FreeSpirit Fabrics**
www.MakeitCoats.com

**Moda Fabrics**
www.ModaFabrics.com

**Timeless Treasures Fabrics**
www.TTFabrics.com

**Windham Fabrics**
www.WindhamFabrics.com

## BATTING

**The Warm Company**
www.WarmCompany.com

## WHAT'S THAT FABRIC?

I used the following fabric collections for some of the quilts in this book:

"Windmills" (page 8): Moon Shine by Tula Pink for FreeSpirit Fabrics

"Half Hitch" (page 11): The Boat House by Sweetwater for Moda Fabrics

"Sunday Best" (page 14): Miss Kate by Bonnie and Camille for Moda Fabrics

"Woodruff" (page 21): Tonga Carnivale by Timeless Treasures Fabrics

"Velocity" (page 24): Mixologie by Studio M for Moda Fabrics

"Pinwheels Plus" (page 36): Color Theory by Vanessa Christenson for Moda Fabrics

"Candy Bracelet" (page 47): Fresh Air by American Jane for Moda Fabrics

"Off Course" (page 51): Terrain by Kate Spain for Moda Fabrics

"Gypsy" (page 54): Various prints designed by Anna Maria Horner for FreeSpirit Fabrics

"Touch a Star" (page 58): Glow by Amy Butler for Westminster Fabrics

"Simplicity" (page 62): Timeless Treasures Basics

"Aviary" (page 65): Up Parasol by Heather Bailey for FreeSpirit Fabrics

## ACKNOWLEDGMENTS

A very sincere thank-you to the following:

**My husband, J.D.,** for his patience and understanding, for not complaining when I was sequestered in my sewing room, and for all the meals, clean laundry, paid bills, and everything else he does to keep me alive and well.

**Karen Williamson,** for years of friendship, for making sample quilts, and for hand-sewing binding when she had more important (and more fun) things to do.

**Linda Jenkins,** my mom, for teaching me to sew, and for a few thousand other things.

**Free Spirit Fabrics, Moda Fabrics, Timeless Treasures Fabrics, and Windham Fabrics** for continuing to offer the most beautiful precut bundles of quality, reliable fabrics that I'm so pleased to use in my quilts.

**The Warm Company** for the luscious batting used in my sample quilts—and the rest of my quilts.

Karen Costello Soltys, Paula Schlosser, Karen Burns, Nancy Mahoney, Tiffany Mottet, Regina Girard, Adrienne Smitke, Cathy Reitan, Brent Kane, and the rest of the talented staff at Martingale for their hard work and professionalism. Working with Martingale is always a delightful experience.

# ABOUT THE AUTHOR

**KIM BRACKETT** lives in Gulf Breeze, Florida, with her husband and a small herd of cats, and works full-time as a paralegal in Pensacola. Kim developed an interest in quilting in 1988 after admiring a collection of vintage quilts displayed in an antique shop. She began gathering tools, fabrics, and patterns and finally finished her first quilt 10 years later. Although she prefers hand quilting, she has overcome many of the challenges of machine quilting and enjoys finishing her quilts in much less time.

Kim has written three other books with Martingale, *Scrap-Basket Surprises*, *Scrap-Basket Sensations*, and *Scrap-Basket Beauties*. She has also contributed her designs to *Sew the Perfect Gift*, *All-Time Favorite Scrap Quilts*, *Perfect Quilts for Precut Fabrics*, and Martingale's yearly wall calendars.

What's your creative passion?
Find it at **ShopMartingale.com**
books • eBooks • ePatterns • daily blog • free projects
videos • tutorials • inspiration • giveaways